WANTING YOU TO WANT ME

WANTING YOU TO WANT ME

Stories from the Secret World of Strip Clubs

Bronwen Parker-Rhodes
and Emily Dinsdale

Hardie Grant

BOOKS

Venus

INTRODUCTION

Strip clubs are worlds within worlds. With their blacked-out windows, burly doormen and the array of complex associations and meanings they carry, strip clubs are, for most people, unexplored or prohibited spaces, walked past on a regular basis but rarely acknowledged or entered.

Within, they are parallel dimensions where the outside world can cease to exist, alternative rules apply and the sense of accelerated intimacy creates unique interactions that don't often occur anywhere else. It's a form of escapism for everyone who enters, punters and strippers alike – an enclave of desire and disappointment. They can be sexually charged environments but, more often than not, the encounters that take place inside have very little to do with sex. Customers and dancers enter a strip club for a range of different reasons.

Wanting You to Want Me is an unflinching insight into this opaque world, narrated by the dancers themselves, most of whom have never spoken publicly about their experiences before. Composed of photographs and stories, it provides personal encounters with the women who work in these sequestered spaces. From vignettes of stripper life to more in-depth narratives, this book allows access to the behind-the-scenes areas of these mysterious venues.

The community of women who work as strippers in these venues exist in the margins, and within this margin are further factions and groups. Women of varied cultural backgrounds from all over the world, with such different experiences of privilege or hardship, are thrown together in an environment that fosters not only conflict and competition but also a strong sense of intimacy and collusion. In the outside world, we may not have otherwise crossed paths, but in the communal space of the changing room, we come together, remove our clothes and, in the process of working alongside one another, often form unique bonds of understanding and shared experience.

Just as every area of London has its own distinct character, so does the culture and atmosphere of every strip venue. They are, each and every one of them, a world unto themselves. But there are overarching similarities we've personally observed, including the overwhelming sense that environments are resistant to change, that they are dominated by formidable women, that any sense of sexual intrigue is often undermined by a kind of vaudevillian camp – a particularly bleak species of black comedy – and that the financial transactions are more complex than a simple exchange of money for nudity.

The constellation of strip clubs in London seems to defy modernity. Whether you're in a down-at-heel, pound-in-the-pot strip pub in the East End or a supposedly sumptuous gentlemen's club up west, there's often something distinctly unmodern about being inside a strip club. Such unambiguous commodification of women's bodies is, or should be, out of date, but strip venues can often feel as hopelessly anachronistic as their decor.

This is a collection of personal stories from our friends and work colleagues with whom we shared changing rooms, stages and podiums. It's accompanied by photographs of dancers, along with scenes and details from various strip venues across London. It's a project we've been working on for several years, trying to find a way to preserve the voices of extraordinary women we've encountered in this disappearing, shifting space.

For better or worse, no other job has ever felt so much like an entire universe. We've experienced the changing landscape in London strip clubs over the past two decades – the advent of private dances, the change from working five girls on a shift to 40 girls per shift, the waves of immigration, the different aspirations of body types, the way the mainstream has embraced pole dancing and how the stigma has lessened over the years in certain enclaves of society. Some of the interviews were conducted during the coronavirus pandemic, when the future of strip clubs was even more uncertain.

As times have changed, we felt an increasing urgency to retain as many of the odd, hilarious, tragic, mundane and compelling stories from within these endangered, cash-in-hand spaces as possible. We are attached to this environment, as dysfunctional and problematic as it may be. Many of the dancers we've spoken to feel the same. Once a stripper, always a stripper.

Though we began collecting these interviews in 2018, they're the product of decades spent working alongside the women we spoke to. They are intimate conversations, not the kind of stories dancers necessarily share with outsiders or civilians. Wherever necessary, we've changed names and redacted locations.

After reaching out to our network of former colleagues on the strip circuit, we recorded their stories as they reminisced about their experiences. Sometimes, they allowed us to take their portraits. Some of the women we spoke to had already given up dancing at the time of sharing their stories, while some were still working as strippers. Some of the interviews were conducted during lockdown, during a unique moment when everybody's feelings about physical proximity to strangers were being re-evaluated.

Many of the photographs – some of which date back to the early 2000s – were taken while working shifts. These images depict the recesses of various venues that would never normally be seen by the public ... the changing rooms, passageways and backstage spaces of the clubs. Some of the portraits correspond with interviews, whereas some of the women we spoke to preferred to remain totally anonymous and would never appear on camera.

We've structured the book by considering the different areas of a club and gathered the stories together based loosely on which space they most occupy most significantly, be it the floor, the stage, the private dance area or the changing rooms.

Although it's by no means definitive, we have included as diverse a range of voices as possible, but there are many women we encountered who don't want their careers in the industry to be documented in any way. There is not one single experience of being a stripper in London and, during a time when attitudes towards sex work feel incredibly polarised, we feel it's important to present these stories in all their ambiguity. We mistrust existing narratives, which seem to oscillate between either fetishising the idea of strippers and sex workers as victims or holding them up as icons of female sexual emancipation. In our experience, the truth is much more complex and nuanced – just one shift working in a strip club can encompass moments of degradation and empowerment. It's also highly subjective and we don't claim to have a monopoly on the 'true' experiences of all strippers, or a definite and clear-cut concept of what being a stripper means in the 21st century. But we have a genuine desire to record the voices and stories of the dancers who are working in the clubs and pubs, many of whom are usually unwilling or unable to speak out about the reality of their work.

Through this collection of candid tales and photographs, we gain privileged access to the secret world of strip clubs. The women who work in and inhabit this mysterious world speak openly to us – recalling the sense of camaraderie (and the feuds) between one another, revealing the truth about their regular customers, and the reality of their lives as dancers – from the bleak comedy and the carnivalesque scenes, to the quietly poignant moments, along with the thrills and the mundanity of performing a version of yourself and your sexuality for a living.

Jade

GISELLE
MISHA
LUCINDA
LOLA
LORELEI
ROXY
KATIE

ON

THE

FLOOR

Whether we're touting a £10 ($14) dance or a champagne-fuelled private party with an extravagant by-the-hour price tag, the floor of the venue is the space where the sales pitch usually begins. What's at stake in every interaction is getting the customer over the threshold into the private dance room for a dance or, even better, up-selling them into a 'sit-down' in the so-called 'VIP' room (in some cases, there's another even more exclusive tier for 'VVIPs' – which you'd be forgiven for thinking is exactly the same experience, but for twice the price). Here, we're selling a luxury product – a kind of sexy companionship with the prospect of intrigue.

The floor of the strip club is a shop floor, it's the place we're most likely to first encounter potential customers. But, if it's a shop floor, it's also a shop window, because we're always on display. We can't afford to totally relax – our shoulders are always thrown back, our stomachs are always sucked in, we're always aware of the customer's gaze and we always have one eye on the door to check who's arriving. We've each assembled our own internal database of customers – we know which girls they tend to dance with, if there's a precedent for them to spend big, if they're time-wasters, if they're good for a drink but not a dance, whether they're a port in a storm.

In between stage shows, we prowl the floor, initiating conversations with customers, gauging their interest, trying to get private dances and hoping to convert them into sit-downs. Or we chat amongst ourselves, drink with the customers, or retreat to the sanctuary of the changing room when we need to replenish our energy. One legendary stripper on the circuit was an unlikely pool shark who, in between her virtuoso performances on the stage, parted customers from more of their money by thrashing them in games of pool. The vision of her in lingerie and six-inch heels, poised over the pool table, cue in hand, is part of London's East End stripper mythology whether you witnessed it or not.

The hustling, in general, is an extension of the stage performance to varying degrees. Out on the floor, even the girls who seem sincere ... well maybe that's part of their persona along with their stage names and costumes. You never really know. Are we putting on an act or are we more ourselves than we've ever previously been allowed to be elsewhere in our lives?

Each venue is its own ecosystem, attracting different types of clientele throughout the course of different hours of the day. The house fee (the money paid to the club by each of the girls for the privilege of working) varies according to how busy each shift tends to be. While there are no hard and fast rules as to who's going to walk through the door, there are inevitable recurring patterns. Daytime shifts (or 'day shafts') in pubs tend to attract pensioners, trades-men who've started work at some unearthly hour of the morning but knocked off early, City boys on long lunch breaks, regulars who've made it their business to pop in for a few dances when their favourite girls are working, and a host of miscellaneous individuals. Nights are more unpredictable, but they still feature their own set of familiar fixtures – the regulars, the seemingly homogenous groups of Essex lads, the work dos, the lone rangers ... but there are often surprises and anomalies.

At the heart of every interaction between a stripper and their client is an exchange of emotional, physical and sexual labour for cash. And to what extent they both choose to acknowledge this is also part of the delicate balancing act. It can be an upfront, transparent transaction or a veiled negotiation. Some dancers are happy talking business, and some can artfully avoid the topic but all the while, the meter is running; it's always running.

Barbara

GISELLE

I wouldn't have gotten into stripping if I hadn't grown up thinking that my beauty was a huge part of my worth. Because I grew up being told a lot, Oh, you're beautiful. And so thinking, *This is an important part of me, my beauty.* So it sort of made sense to go and capitalise on that because, obviously, this is who I am – beautiful. You keep telling yourself, *I don't care what they say.* But a bit of you does; a bit of you does get some validation from being praised all the time. And then I think it sort of compounds itself, because a lot of my sense of self-worth was tied up with my appearance.

I think my idea of beauty was very standardised, just sort of like, there is one way to look beautiful and it is to be slim but not skinny, and to have long hair and smooth, tanned skin. I wouldn't like to admit that, I would have liked to think I'm someone who really sees the beauty in variety and in difference but, honestly, I don't think I did believe that.

When I started dancing I was just 18 and terrified of being found out. Outwardly, I think I was quite a well-behaved sort of girl, and I was scared of getting in trouble. I went to Oxford [University] and I was scared of being chucked out. That was a very real thing. Also, my dad – I was just always scared of my dad. I was scared he would somehow find out, even though he lived in another country. So I think I just really wanted to protect myself and stay very anonymous.

At my audition I had no understanding, as an 18-year-old, of just how inherently sexy and desired you are. Like, you don't need to do anything else other than be 18 and female. The society we live in prizes youth and all I needed to do was walk in there go, Hi, I've got tits. And they would've given me a job. But in no way did I understand that. I thought I had to create some elaborate, sexy persona. So I became French. That was my thing. So for some reason when I walked in – it's so ridiculous – but, yeah, 18-year-old me walks into the club and says, 'Ello, I am 'ere for zee interview. In this comedic, breathy French accent. Or something along those lines. And they're like, Right love, what's your name? I said, Giselle. It happened to be the name of the character in the book I was reading at the time, because I was studying French at uni and so, yeah, I'd got this nailed.

I've always had a bit of a fucked accent because of growing up internationally, and it got way worse from working at the club. I would be talking to people from college and they'd be like, What's happening with your voice? I'd sort of like forget what person I was meant to be. It was really awkward. And then, after eight months of that it got really, really hard. Because I was living in Oxford and commuting, there were some nights I ended up staying the night after work. I made friends with a couple of the girls and stayed at their place. And so they're, you know, they're lending me pyjamas and they're feeding me and I'm still going, Thank you. Zis is so kind of you, I feel like we are really friends now. Somehow I'd sort of Frenched myself into a corner.

I always put on so many different facades for different scenarios and that's something I did from being very little as well. So it was something that came quite naturally. Massive daddy issues there, because I think a big part of it was I always played a role for him, to please him. Textbook.

There was one girl who had been really kind to me – she ended up being, I feel bad saying, she ended up being a fucking nightmare. She was a 'character'. But she was really, really nice to me at the beginning. So I told her. We were walking between two different clubs because we had a split shift and I said, Trudi, I 'ave something to say to you ... I'm not French. And she was just dying laughing. I'd been so nervous. I was sweating, I was like, I've got to come clean. But she found it really funny.

As it was, I kept it up for the full 15 years, just from that one day going in and saying 'Ello, I'm called Giselle. For 15 years I had people thinking I was French. I still do – there are still people out there who think I'm French.

· ·
·

I think it's important to say that when people were just out-and-out knobs I didn't tolerate it. When you're underestimated by a customer in a way that is cruel and shows their own misogyny, at that point the persona of being sexy was forgotten and the persona of being much smarter came out. Which was just like, *I know I can absolutely destroy you with my mind.* And I really enjoyed that because, obviously, you're in such a position of power there because they're always on the back foot. They never expect you to be really fucking smart. So immediately they're at a disadvantage because they've seen you in one particular way, to then have to sort of recalibrate and see you differently, they're blindsided, like, Shit, you were just some tits on perspex shoes a minute ago and now, argh, a personality.

You can cut people down with total impunity in the club. If they do anything to you, you know, you could say something that cuts to the quick of them, really sort of, *I see exactly who you are, you feeble being, and I'm totally going to cut you down.* And if you said that to them in the street they'd probably be so destroyed that they'd hit you, they'd do something, they'd hurt you. But you can't be hurt in there.

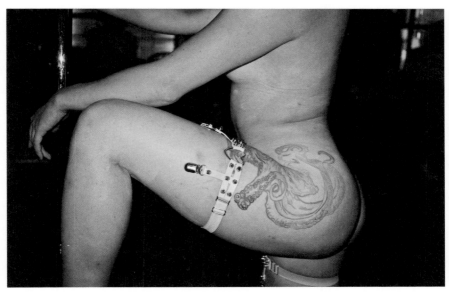

Jade

MISHA

When I started working at ████████, they already had a girl there with my real name so I couldn't use it. So I said I wanted something sophisticated but a bit bitchy and, like, something you don't hear a lot. It's actually a Russian man's name, but yeah, I'm Misha. Sometimes I forget my real name. Misha is a completely different person, like 360 degrees. If someone calls me Misha, I change completely, I'm not sweet anymore, I'm bitchy.

I've been dancing for three years, but with the quarantine, let's say two. Since I was 18 and three months exactly. I needed the money. I came to this country with only £100 ($140), and I stayed with the cousin of my ex-boyfriend. In one week I paid one month's rent, a month's deposit, plus the money I owed for the week's rent. I mean, I knew my goal – I just wanted to escape.

I didn't ever really fancy dancing, even though I'm a good dancer. I like to go to clubs, party and stuff, but the first time was horrible, like, completely horrible. I started crying. I didn't even do an audition because I'm late all the time to work, I can't be on time, it's a big problem. So they didn't give me an audition, they just put me straight away to work. The audition was when it was full of customers, like *full* full. They told me to take off my bra and dance and spin on the pole. I was like, Hell no. And I start crying on the stage. The men were like, No, leave her alone! And then the house mum – fucking bitch – she's like, No, she has to do this, it's her job.

My first private dance was after one month and a half of working as a dancer, because I hadn't been trying to get private dances. I was just having drinks with the customers, and talking in the VIP area, but nothing else. I was drinking Champagne, which was actually Prosecco from Tesco – the shittest one, like, the worst, £3 ($4) a bottle. And because my body got used to the Prosecco, I had to drink whisky shots so I could get drunk.

The first time I did a private dance was horrible. I didn't take my under-wear off. The house mum, she came inside the private dance and said, You have to take them off. Then they kicked out the customer from the private dance and took off my underwear without him seeing it. Yeah, it was horrible. I nearly beat her up, she was very aggressive. But later, she saw I was making the most money in there because I was the youngest one, so she had to be nice with me.

I stayed at that place for six or seven months. For the first three, four months I was just working, working, working, then I start to see that they were stealing money from me. You see, the customers pay the money to the club, and at the end of the night they give us a part of that money if it's cash, if not, they write it in a book and pay you later. But in the meantime, the glasses of champagne – they were taking the money from them as well and not giving me a cut. You know, like they forgot to put it in the notebook, but I was remembering how many I had because I'm not stupid. I came there for money, you know, I didn't come to have fun. Like, hell, no. So after that I was staying just at the tables with the customers making just tips for myself – £400, £500 ($550, $700) a night – but for the club I was making fuck all. But they keep me because they couldn't say anything, the customers were coming just to drink with me because I was the youngest one there. The second one after me, she was 35 years old at the time. So, I was there, 18 years old. I'm brand new, I was like a doll. Now I'm a cow.

When I started in the beginning, I didn't speak English. Like, fuck all. I was kind of shy, I couldn't understand, I couldn't speak no words. I learned to speak English with the customers. They taught me, they were like professors. And then it was amazing when I started speaking English, it was more money, more fun. Now I can go with every guy, I just have to be in the mood. I'm, how to say ... I adapt. If you cry now, I'm crying with you. Like, I make it so real sometimes I believe it myself. Since I started to work, they explained to me, you have to be like them, you have to interact, to work with your face. You laugh, I laugh, you know, I'm like this.

When I'm with a customer, I'm always smiling like a baby, even if I don't feel like it, I can't help it. And most of the other girls, they're old. You know the type of girls they have at ███████, and they don't treat the customers the right way. They're like, begging for money. And me, I don't beg. The English girls are just dickheads. Sorry for that, but, oh my god, English people are the worst. They are, like, so lazy. They take everything for granted, you know? Because they think, Oh, I'm British I deserve this, this is all mine. And I'm like, *No, it's actually mine.*

In the summer of 2019, I was the top girl. I was working every day starting at 12 o'clock, finishing one in the morning. I was telling the guys I was 29, I got three kids and have a degree in psychology, and I even started to believe it. Then when I went back home to see my mum, I told her like, Yeah, I'm going to be 30 next year. She was like, What?! But you know, I'd been telling that every day to people, so you start believing it. I was going home and feeling old. And it took me like three, four months just to feel like myself again.

I started to tell the guys I was older because I look really young. Even now, if I lose some weight, I look really, really young, even if I put makeup on. They would say, No, you're too young for me. And I'd say, No, I'm 30! And I'd know what year to say my birthday is, what star sign, everything. Most of them, they were like my grumpy great, great, great grandpa.

∴

Six months before lockdown, I fucked up my life. Through dancing I met this girl Johanna. She's a drug addict, and I went a bit in that way. At the time I was making money just to buy more drugs. Then, after one year, I said, *Fuck it. I'm not going to do it anymore.* That's why I'm a fat cow now, because I didn't used to eat. But still, I was making good money and sending it back home to my family to help them.

Some of my regular customers have been helping me through lockdown. One, he's American, he has been helping me for the last two years with the rent, money for food and everything. He thinks he's my boyfriend and I'm in love with him. I met him at ▬▬▬▬▬. At the start we were friends, then he broke up with a girl he was in a relationship with. She was a dancer as well, but a bitch one – a Romanian too. She took advantage of him, and he didn't know because he was madly in love. After they break up he starts speaking to me again and I saw an opportunity and took it.

I was always tough. Even when I first came here I wasn't like a little lamb, I came strong. I had to toughen myself up because of family problems I had before. So when I came out here I was prepared. I have six brothers so you can imagine how many times they beat me up. So I don't take no bullshit. I said to my mum when I came here, I'm a bartender, a waitress, a cleaner … but she didn't buy it, she knew I was lying. After two weeks she told me, I know you're a dancer, why are you lying to me? I know you're doing something dodgy.

I learn so many things from being a stripper, especially how to lie the best. How you can lie to people so much you even start believing it yourself. That's the first lesson and the worst one someone can learn, how to lie. I've also learnt that people are fucking cunts, like 99 per cent of people and humanity are cunts. I hate people. I love animals though. In 10 years' time I'd like to be taking care of animals in Madagascar. I want to go to the Amazon and travel the world. I don't know if I'm going to have any kids but, if I do, of course, they're not going to end up like me, doing the same mistakes. I'm going to take better care of them than my parents did, for sure, 100 per cent.

Honestly, for me, to be a dancer it takes a lot of courage. A lot of courage to focus and do what you do. I'm not a dancer because it's fun. You just have to be brave and believe in yourself, and just focus, focus on the money not on the people. People say, Oh you didn't do anything powerful in your life, and I say, Yeah, I do *many* powerful things in my life – I'm a stripper.

LUCINDA

I grew up in an all-female household where the idea of feminism was just to talk about how men are shit and all they do is think with their penises. I don't subscribe to that. I came to dancing quite late, I couldn't have done it in my twenties. I was 38, which is when most people stop. And I promised myself when I started dancing – if I start to despise men for their sexuality, I want to stop.

Well, my stripper name is Lucinda. Ages ago, when I lived in California, my aunt had this pristine 1989 Toyota Corolla. It ended up going to my cousin, but then he gave it to me. I was driving over the Bay Bridge one time, and the car overheated and I completely fucked it. It died a horrible death. I had nicknamed the car Lucinda, so when I was thinking, *What am I gonna call myself?* I thought, *I'll go with Lucinda so that car will live on.*

Lucinda tries to stay in the sweet, caring zone – affectionate and welcoming. I try to give good customer service and not really bitch and moan about myself. That doesn't always work, but I try to maintain that. I just treat everybody as if they're quality, you know, whether they're a dustbin man or a banker.

When I first started dancing, I was so clueless. I wasn't a natural born stripper at all. I was going through some heavy shit in my life and I was quite broken, really. It took me almost two years before I started making money, but I was going through some really crazy shit. So, yeah, I was definitely very unconfident and had an inferiority complex. It took me ages to get out of my own self-absorption and just sort of be like, *No, it's about them and making them feel good.* When I'm on-point at work, I'm in this sweet spot where I'm flirty just enough, even though, you know, I'm sort of a little bit bland as a person. Like, you still have your core, you know who you are, but it's about fitting in.

I have always been pretty short on cash and had financial constraints. So I've never been able to spend loads on amazing outfits.

When I first started I was just wearing kind of hand-me-downs and things I'd bought cheaply. A customer actually said to me once, Look, you're an older woman, you should go for classy and not slutty. So I sort of moved into that style and, you know, you can see in people's visual reaction to you what things accentuate you right. You can tell which are money-making outfits and which aren't. And it can just be like a reflex thing of how this shape lights up that circuit in their brain, and that shape doesn't. For me, it's basically about the cello shape, the in and the out of the midriff. So I like things that accentuate my waist. I suppose, these days it's also about covering up what I don't want to show 'cause I'm older and I'm aware of my skin.

. .
.

When I first started it was like, *Whoa, this is sexual sensory overload* – because I was in a very high-contact club. I've realised now that I have to stay away from that, partly because you get desensitised and partly because it actually damages me. I think for a while there I was a bit of a naughty dancer – not major naughty, but a bit naughty. Now, I think my USP – unique selling point – is that I make people feel welcomed and respected and kind of warm and loved. And nothing fazes me. Like, you can tell me any of your sexual fantasies and I just don't say shit. You know, I don't judge. I'm happy to talk about any kind of sexual thing, nothing bothers me like that. More and more I've wanted to steer away from, Oh, can I lick your nipples? and that kind of thing, and more to, Hey, let's just go and have a giggle and a cuddle. Or maybe, like, lap-dances that are role plays.

I've got this little whip that I bought and these fake glasses. I'm not really allowed to use them at my club, but I will quite often put them on and I'll be like, Do you like to be dominant or submissive? And then my kind of go-to scenario will be like, I'm either the secretary or the boss. And it's actually just a lap dance, but with a lot of chat. It gives a space for guys to try BDSM as an experience and see if they like it. Oh, you've never been submissive? Okay, well do you want me to kick you in the balls or do you want to walk around and be my dog? Most dancers I know love guys who want to get kicked in the balls.

I really don't think guys just come in for tits and ass – I think people come in for escapism. I've had lap dances where it's just total silliness and there's nothing sexy about it at all. It takes the pressure off 'cause the thing is, if you've got a half-hour VIP and you're just bouncing up and down on someone's lap and grazing your nipples past their face they're going to get really horny, and then it's this tug of war between you trying to maintain your boundaries and the club's rules, and them wanting to fuck you. If you do something different where you take their energy in a different way, you can get around that issue. Unless they're like a tantric practitioner no one can be really turned on for half an hour without wanting to get rid of some of that energy.

I had this argument with my current boss because he doesn't get that, you know. He got very, very angry with me. He shouted at me in front of customers. Once I had this guy crawling around on his hands and knees licking my heel, and the manager came and he screamed at me. It was very embarrassing and completely killed the vibe – the guy didn't spend any more after that. And the manager, he's like, Just a normal lap dance!

I think, for me, my biggest challenge with stripping has been dealing with the managers. That's probably the most unforeseen, detrimental part of this whole chapter in my life. Bear in mind, I used to be a business journalist. I've had other careers; I've worked in a range of other environments. The lack of business discipline in this industry is very frustrating, especially when it comes as a personal assault. The mind games, the manipulation, the abuse, the threatening, people fucking with you – like really fucking with you! It's just the unfairness of it all. It's been a really good insight into what it's like to be a marginalised person in society. I mean, fucking hell the amount of scorn and anger I have about it. And it frustrates me because I think this is a really viable industry, but especially in the UK, the management for the most part has just been full of fucking idiots.

People who should not have power are given power. Also, there's the dynamic of you being naked and them being clothed. I think that power stuff goes on in every sphere of every kind of management. You know, you have to be a very self-aware, well-trained manager to not succumb to that ego trip. But I think the main thing is that strippers are in the closet and we haven't had organising power – until now.

·· ·

I get on with everybody, but I have always clicked with working men. You know, for instance, I worked at ███████ in Southend. It's gone now, but there were not a lot of missing teeth in that place. There was a lot of guys coming in in work clothes, and you know what? They were respectful, they were straightforward, they were appreciative, and I got on great with them. I mean, I can get on with all kinds of customers but I just find that their behaviour is a bit different in a pub. Maybe it's just 'cause there's not as much coke.

What I've loved about dancing is the conversations; that, actually, men can be incredibly soulful. I remember this guy saying to me, The porn I love is of women who've had loads of kids and their tits are like empty sacks and their pussies are stretched out, that's the porn I love. So there's an amazing variety of what people are into sexually, you know, so a lot of very varied conversations. Also, I love learning about people's lives, 'cause I really do try to relate, you know. Like last night, I was talking about bricks with a bricklayer and I never knew that there were so many different kinds of bricks, but I've learned stuff like that through stripping.

I don't think all guys are shits and, like, there are lots of guys who come to strip clubs because they're trying to be faithful to their wife and they don't want to have sex with anyone else, but they just miss affection. You have guys who say, You don't need to take your knickers off. You know, they're not really there for that. It's almost like the energy of having a naked body next to you, which we all need hormonally; we need the oxytocin. So you know, you can never judge.

I was thinking about this recently. My customers, I sort of see them like plants – I try to tend to them. I check in with them, I check they're alright, I try to remember their birthdays – shit like that. I do really love my customers, my regulars. I'm not *in* love with them or anything like that but, you know, you do need to nurture the relationship.

I mean, I suppose with any customer relationship you have to nurture it, you have to make deposits as well as making withdrawals.

⁘

You're not an underclass, but you are an outlaw class. And your relationships with the other girls, it's accelerated. Because you've seen each other's pussies, you've like, pretended to lick them out. You've probably peed in front of each other, changed a tampon in front of each other. I've been fortunate in that some of the places where I've worked the longest, there's been a really nice vibe with the girls. Friendships do ebb and flow, but I've definitely got some lifelong friends through dancing.

Once I sort of found my feet as a stripper, I just wanted to be appreciative of all the other women. They've all got something beautiful, you know, physically or in terms of their manner or whatever, and I'm not going to see them as competition. There's always those girls who are just so fucking gorgeous you can't help but feel like Mrs. Diddly Squat next to them. Especially if you're someone like me, you know, I'm just your normal height brunette, but sometimes you're working with a model type who's just eye-wateringly gorgeous. But I try not to let that turn into a competitive vibe. I try not to get into that kind of thinking, where you try to make yourself feel better by telling yourself like, *Yeah she's gorgeous but, I mean, look at her arse* ... I try not to do that.

I'm 46 now. I think stripping's probably been a bit negative for me, really, in that it's made me quite panicky about ageing. I mean, I think there's a point where you have to kind of watch your dignity, even if you're still making money. But, up until that point, guys don't really give a shit. You're either their type or you're not. And I'm not even talking about visual type, there's a wide range of ways you can be their type. So they don't really give a shit, you know. That's how I feel about it.

I remember this woman in my first club, she'd been stripping for years, she was a club stripper and she would have made money in a morgue. She also had an amazing look – natural, beautiful boobs and just a beautiful woman. And I remember she was like, Look, you could honestly wear a black plastic bag – it's 10 per cent how you dance, 10 per cent what you say, and 80 per cent your energy. I mean, that's true about everything really, but I think in stripping it's partly because your audience is generally inebriated so they're working more on an energetic level. So their cognitive mind is disabled – not in a bad way, I'm not saying they're going to go around and rape every-one or lose their moral compass, because I fucking hate that narrative too, but you know what I mean.

Do I have any plans to quit? I mean, I've wound it down. I was working five days a week and now I just dance two days a week. For the last three Christmases I've told myself I'm going to quit. And those deadlines all sailed past me and it's just created so much stress. So now I've decided, you know what? It'll end when it's ready. And I'm not going to stress about it.

∙ ∙

My whole mindset has been an attitude of gratitude. I'm not going to pour scorn on the customers. If there were strip clubs for women like me, I would go to them. Not all the time but, why not? It's just a bit of fun. And, when I've been single, it would probably have been really good for me to go and have just a bit of male attention. So I never, never want to talk shit about the customers. I never want to bitch about them. I really, really try not to. I try not to laugh at their sexual idiosyncrasies. I mean, there is this guy that comes in and talks about how his real fantasy is getting a milk enema and then drinking the poo milk, and, like, you know, that is quite stomach-turning. But that's his thing. And, you know, he's a very respectful guy, he's not trying to force his shit on you. I just do not believe in looking down on different sexual interests, as long as it's legal and consensual.

People are always asking me questions about the job, like, You must meet some real weirdos? And it really irritates me and I kind of feel like saying, *No, you're the one who's being the weirdo right now, because you're being so prurient about it*. Why have we got this thing that strippers must be damaged or without choice and that customers must be broken rejects. No, you have such a range of reasons why guys come in and a lot of them can be very healthy reasons. You know what I mean?

I just think we need to celebrate consensual, legal, sexual entertainment and keep it at that. I think it's so valuable in many ways. You know, you get Hasidic Jews next to Muslims, next to punk rockers, criminals next to judges. You know, and they probably even have a laugh with each other. It's a leveller isn't it? I love that.

Vagas

LOLA

Fantasy! Fantasy is the biggest commodity. You and the customer are complicit in building this fantasy about things you could do *if only*.

The customers definitely get to act out being the kind of man they want to be – someone who is supporting you, fulfilling this saviour complex. Especially in the money that they're spending, they want to know that it's going towards your personal development; that, in this very patriarchal way, they're able to save you and support you in your struggle. Not exactly a father figure but somewhere along those lines. It makes them feel important and needed. I never went as far as pretending that I was studying but that's a good one.

.·.

I started to notice that I didn't want to talk to anyone after I'd been working. After having been at work making conversation with people and putting so much energy into entertaining them, there was nothing left for going into another bar as a civilian and talking to strangers and telling them about my life, because I had been doing that all day. You start seeing *all* social interaction as a performance of some sort. Ever since I reached a point of burnout with dancing, I only really want to be surrounded by my inner circle, and I don't really have much energy for going out and presenting myself to a room full of strangers. But a positive side of it, I suppose, was that it made me realise how much I perform.

I think it was only by explicitly performing that I realised how many areas of life we're also performing in all the time. I also realised how much I performed sexuality in everyday life. And, as a result of that, I started re-evaluating how I behave in my intimate life and the way that we conform to others' expectations without really realising it. You're so scared to disappoint someone in your private life, and this has been actually the most valuable thing to realise. This job helps you set these boundaries because you learn how to say no. If someone's not paying or if they're not worth your time then they're not getting it anymore. And that level of boundaries, of confidence – of sass! – can be quite affirming outside as well.

It's about taking the expectations people have of women and re-evaluating them – that a woman is expected to be happy, attentive, nurturing. And that's something that's imposed on us, but it's also something we can take advantage of and replicate in the club environment. It's somewhere where men can purchase it, whereas perhaps outside, women are not going to be patient and smile at them, thinking they're interesting. So, are we reproducing those values, expectations, clichés, by working in this environment? Or are we actually destroying that by making it a commodity?

I find it so inconceivable now when I see these lingerie shops and think of wives going in there to buy this lingerie to look sexy for their husbands. All the elaborate bras you can't actually wear under clothes, they're meant to be worn on their own. You're just offering yourself up as a gift! In the context of stripping or sex work that's completely legitimate because you're getting paid for it. Before I started stripping, perhaps I didn't question it so much. But now, something about it would make me feel weird – presenting yourself as a gift in lingerie to a man you're striving for genuine intimacy with? We'll leave that kind of performance in the strip club. That's the kind of empowerment you get out of this job.

I don't know what to do with my lingerie now that I've stopped dancing. As I was leaving work, I sold a lot of it to the other girls. They were asking about particular pieces and I was joking, Oh, I'm saving that for my wedding night. And they thought I was serious! But I'm still saving it for *something* – I'm not sure what that is, and there are times when I completely want to burn it all and get it out of my life and not have that around anymore. But I think I'm keeping it because there's value in the material objects, in the way that they represent those memories and the lessons that I've learnt from it. But, you know, maybe I'm just keeping it to one day show my kids!

It was very rare that a customer actually started to creep me out. There was just one really sad old man with certain fetishes that just made him seem weak and despicable. He had this crazy home situation because he had a younger wife who loved making him the cuckold. And he would put up with this because it meant he got to have a young wife with pretty legs. But sometimes he would come in and he'd be really upset about it. Then, in order to make himself feel better, he'd want to just stare at your vagina. After a while, that started really getting to me, you know, because he would tell you his story, he'd tell you his whole life and, at some point, I just wanted to kick him and say, Sort yourself out. Have a bit of dignity or self-respect.

Venus

LORELEI

It's a world. It's a fake world. But the longer you work there, the more you understand it. You get to know the people more, the regulars. They're the ones who create the world in their minds more than anyone, we join in because it's how we make our living.

We're fantasy technicians. That's what it is. I do believe that. I wouldn't lie, but I would spare parts of myself, like having a partner and stuff. They'd be like, I bet you partied yesterday. I'm not going to tell them that I just got up early and went to do a gym class or took my kid to nursery.

People used to come and ask you, Where are you from? And I'm like, Hey, where do you want me to be from? And I'll go with it, it doesn't matter. But yeah, I think that job did teach me a lot about mens' worlds. In the beginning I thought, *Oh, it's all about big boobs and blonde hair.* But I've learned over the years it's a lot because they're lonely and they want to talk to someone.

.. .

Coming back to work after having a baby ... You come from this poop-filled nappy changing, breastfeeding world to *this*. All this, it felt unreal, like, *This is what I do?!* And it really felt crazy. Like, I come from, you know, the life of *that* situation, then you have to sit and listen to all the girls talking about nail varnish and their eyebrows. It was hard to leave the baby as well. But I learned to really love and appreciate these nonsense moments with my girls ... to dress up, to feel sexy – which you don't do day in and day out at home with your kid – and to enjoy the silly chats.

My first shift after having the baby ... Oh my God, it was nerve-wracking. You feel out of place. You can't believe ... I don't know. It took me a couple of weeks to get used to it. With my body, I mean,

I was quite lucky, it wasn't too bad. By the time I came back, it was fine. My boobs dropped two sizes, which was really heartbreaking because I was quite proud of my boobs before. They weren't horrible after, but they didn't have that 'wow' effect anymore. They had just shrunk, the baby sucked the life out of them. Then I got customers saying, Oh yeah, but we want someone with boobs. I got comments like that. And I was like, Fine.

Babe, listen, if I had loads of money, I'm not even going to lie, I would get it all done. I still dream of a nose job and thigh gap. I'm dying to do my nose and I will be doing my boobs. I'm saving it for my 40th – a pick-me-up 'cause I'm sure I'm going to cry on my 40th birthday.

Natural? Excuse me. No, I'm not paying for a boob job for them to look natural. No, no, no, no. They look natural now. I mean, when I get them done, I would want to make sure they're not wonky. 'Cause we've seen a lot of those in our job, right? But this is the only thing that would potentially bother me. Otherwise, what am I paying all this money for? To sag? Nah, wait for age, that will do it on its own. After pregnancy or age, they will drop further. To be honest, it's only at our job that we care about what it looks like bare because, in your life, only you and your partner see it. So all you care about is what it looks like in clothes. The only time I'll say I want to look natural is when it comes to my face. Anything else, I don't care. I still want the thigh gap. I don't care if you're going to think it's natural or not.

I think having a kid actually made me more money. I know it sounds strange. I was very careful when I came back not to talk about the kid, never to say anything because, you know, you don't want to start talking to customers about your kids, it's a put-off. You want to sell the fantasy and all that. But, the funny thing is, most people that come to the club are fathers, married men who are a bit bored, people who are lonely. If it's someone young I'm not going to say anything, but here and there, I would talk about it – I've always been quite honest and wasn't good at the BS thing. Because, you know, they told us about everything. They'd be like, I have a little girl. And I'm like, Oh congratulations. How old is yours? They're 12 months old. And I'd say, Oh, I've got a 12-month-old boy. And the second you say that it's like a conversation starter – from nappies (diapers) to nursery, they even ask me advice on how they can be more supportive to their wife. I used to say, Trust me, if you go and get her coffee in the morning and flowers, she's going to love you to the end of time for doing that silly something. Because that's all she wants right now – a coffee and a hug. Or they'd say, like, It's so hard for me because the kid just wants his mum. And I'd tell them, I know, but it's a phase and you have to kind of push through it. And it continues, so on.

. .
.

Would I describe myself as a person of faith? Yeah. I do, I do believe. I mean, just because you're stripping doesn't mean you don't have faith. Some people would disagree. But everyone has a different view on faith. I mean, it's quite funny to see someone getting smashed on a Saturday night and then she posts on Facebook about going to church on Sunday. It is funny, it's very amusing. But at the same time, it doesn't mean you can't be a stripper and still have religion.

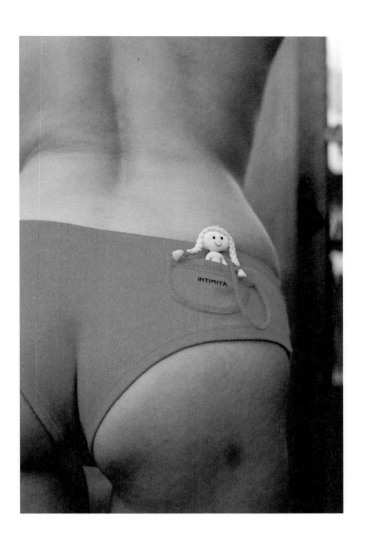

ROXY

Right now I'm doing the nursing thing, I'm a local dental nurse. Which I'm very lucky to do, but God, I'm working so hard for my money! Obviously at the moment [during the Pandemic] I need to do it but I work with dentists for eight, nine hours, and I'm just thinking, *My God, the money that I'm making there all day, I used to make this same money in literally 20 minutes.* It's just so hard to downgrade. Seriously. So I'm actually so very grateful that I was a dancer. I met so many amazing girls and we still keep in touch. Most of my best friends I actually met through dancing, otherwise I don't even know how you can make friends because normal people ... most of them are so bloody boring, I can't relate to them whatsoever. I'm just thinking, *Thank God that was not my whole life*, you know. Twenty years altogether probably I was dancing, and I think every single dancer says the same thing, they never in a million years regret it. It was an amazing opportunity for travel, friends and money.

One hundred per cent, I was a lot more myself as a dancer. Because they let you be yourself, you know? They let you choose when you want to work, what you want to wear, who you want to approach ... there's a lot of freedom. But where I'm working now, you're like a slave basically. You can't be yourself because no one cares about your opinion. I don't even exist as a nurse. When the people come in, they don't even say hi to me, or thank you, or goodbye. I'm like a ghost in the surgery. Whereas there, I was a queen. I got a lot of attention, and I had choices. If I don't like something that you say I can just walk away. Whereas when you're working in the surgery with the same people eight, nine hours a day, even if they're rude to you, you bloody have to continue. So, sometimes, I really want to tell them to fuck off. But obviously this is not the world where you can say that. Whereas, when you're dancing, you can be yourself, you can tell them to fuck off. So, yeah, I was totally, one hundred per cent more myself when I was a dancer. Now, I have to pretend really.

I was never acting as a dancer – I never even changed my name. At first I was using my own name because I was proud of what I was doing. Obviously I changed it when I started nursing. I changed it to Roxy because I thought it was best to be a little bit more incognito with all the social media stuff.

· ·
·

Obviously, some of the guys are very, very rude to us. Sometimes you need to approach 10 or 20 guys on your own and you have to listen to all these silly comments. You've got small tits, you're too fat, you're too skinny, you're too old, or they don't like Eastern European girls … and you just need to stand there, looking beautiful and confident and sometimes it's really hard to just take all these nasty things. But you need to rise above it because you've got another three more hours to go and you need the money. You have to build this bulletproof thing throughout the years, but sometimes it gets to you.

I'm all natural. Apart from my Botox, my lips, fillers and stuff like that. But that's because of ageing I started to do that, to maintain myself. But otherwise, I haven't done anything. I have a bit of a belly, but whatever, I've inherited it from my family. Even when I do a lot of exercise I still have a bit of a belly. And sometimes they ask me, Oh, are you pregnant? Stuff like that. They just want to be nasty sometimes. I don't know how that is going to make them feel good, but I think sometimes they just want to put you down and be rude to you.

As I got older I changed how I was with the customers a little bit. When you're younger you look better and, you know, they go for that look. But as I got older I stopped leading so much with my looks. Obviously I'm trying to maintain a good look in there, you know, do your hair and nails and everything. But I think I've become more of a friend with elderly customers because they're not just looking at you, they like you as a person. So I was making money with customers that actually wanted my company. They wanted to have a good conversation, they wanted someone to have a little bit of care for them. I would remember what they told me last time, if they went to horse racing or stuff like that, and I'd ask them about it. They all love that sort of thing. I kind of became friends with them, and because we became friends, that's why they pay for my time. And, obviously, they wanted to see me naked as well but, being older, I think I became more of a company dancer instead of just taking my clothes off and them wanting to see me inside out. I got a little bit more respect 'cause I was older.

• •
•

I was a terrible dancer. I was awful. The other girls showed me a few times what to do, how you climb up on a pole and stuff, but it was a disaster. Every time I had to go on stage, especially if I was after some of these amazing dancers like Joy or Chiqui, I'm thinking, *Shall I go on or not?* Because the customers are probably going to be so disappointed with what I'm doing. But I'd think, *Fuck it, have another drink and let's just get it over with.* Oh God, I hated the stage. It's really something, you know, to stand out there in front of all those people looking at you and performing. We were actually really brave if you think about it, don't you think? Really, babe, in the City of London, you get on stage and just take everything off. Four minutes completely naked in front of all these people. I would not want to do it again now. I'm done.

I always admired the other girls and what they do, but I was never a good dancer, that's not how I make my money. I show that I'm interested in their day or what they do, stuff like that. I'm not always interested, you can't be interested for four hours with every single person, but you have to kind of look interested, you know, or you pay them compliments, stuff like that. Try to find things in common. I was always looking for something that they were happy to talk about and I'd just hang onto that and make them feel good. And then when we feel like we have a bit of a connection – bang, we go for a dance and I get your money.

You learn how to read people, and I applied that skill to my nursing as well. I mean, I take no bullshit from anyone. I don't give a shit about them. I've got no feelings for any of the deadbeats that I'm working with, I never let them walk all over me. And that's why they quite like me because I do my job properly and I'm confident.

Throughout my 20 years, I would meet so many different characters in one day. A lot more than the average girl. I have one best friend, and the number of guys she's meeting in one year, I met that in four hours. So I read them like a book. With their body language, the things they say, I just know them all. But don't get me wrong, I love the boys anyway, and it hasn't changed my mind about them. It's just funny how much they lie to get into your pants. It just makes me laugh. I look at my friend and I'm thinking, *God, I have so much experience*, but maybe that's why I'm single – because I have *too* much experience, I know too much.

I stopped last year and I'm 46 now. So let's say 44, I stopped. That's quite late for a dancer. And you know what? I never thought I'd even dance after 30, but the time was so good and so much fun, 10 years just went like that. When I got to 40 I was like, *Roxy, this is ridiculous, what are you doing!?* But it was still good, I still looked good, I still felt good. But now I would not want to take my clothes off.

Presley

Presley

Presley

KATIE

People were always really interested when I told them I was a stripper. People are curious about what actually takes place inside strip clubs. Maybe they imagine a really heightened erotic atmosphere, saturated with sex. But, in my experience, sex is demystified in a strip club – you can buy a striptease just the same as you can buy a packet of roasted peanuts or a drink. It's just another thing for sale.

I often found it quite comical there, like a 1970s sitcom. At Christmas time you would sometimes find yourself performing a striptease to something really inappropriate, like that Band Aid song, 'Do They Know It's Christmas?' And I'd always laugh to myself because it was so absurd, but I'd look around and it was as if no one else noticed it was funny.

They installed big plasma-screen televisions, but often they'd be showing like, *The Great British Bake Off* while girls were performing stripteases on stage and, on daytime shifts, bar staff would sometimes heat their lunch up in a microwave behind the bar and you could smell, like, chicken korma or chilli con carne. There's something about the smell of hot food – especially hot meat – that's so incongruous with sex. It's such a school dinner odour.

It wasn't slick. One night there was a power cut. There was a load of roadwork on ████████ Road and they must've damaged some cables; the whole area was in blackout. It was a Saturday night – the busiest night – so there was no question of closing early. They set up a noisy generator to power the music and someone got hold of one of those industrial-type spotlights you get on building sites. It cast this really unforgiving, crude light on the stage that we all looked awful in, but there was a Blitz spirit about just carrying on regardless.

There's definitely something gladiatorial about walking out of the changing room and into the club, especially on a Friday or Saturday night. And feeling bonded to the girls because you're united in the sense that you have a common enemy and a common goal. It's like being with your unit in the army and being sent on a military tour of duty. Because often you're with women you have very little in common with, culturally, and sometimes you only have a little bit of shared language, but you have this currency that you both understand of, like, awful customers, shit shifts, and you just have to laugh.

Also, I mean, you've seen each other naked and contorted in all sorts of weird positions – you've seen *up* each other. You're sharing mirrors and one girl is applying mascara and eating a pho soup while you're next to her inspecting your vagina – literally opening it up and poking around – to check there's no toilet paper residue. All in the same mirror. And that is very levelling.

**HARMONY
POPPY
CHIQUI
BEX
CLEO**

ON

STAGE

Venus

Whether on the stage or in the private room, the dance itself pivots on the interplay between exposure and concealment. We can draw out that moment of suspense as long as we wish; we can luxuriate in it, prolonging each gesture as if it's dragged through honey. Or we can be swifter and find the drama in a more immediate reveal – all strip and no tease.

There's often an element of exchange, whereby our performance is affected by the audience – how busy it is in the club, the atmosphere, how generously customers are with their applause (and their cash), etcetera. Our stage routine is performed for the pleasure of the viewer; we are courtesans and geishas interpreting our audience's desires. Or not. Maybe we're dancing purely for our own enjoyment, enacting our own fantasy of ourselves, and the customers are just our props or extras. They're the meat in the room.

We are both subject and object, watching ourselves being watched; watching them watching us.

When a venue doesn't offer private dances, we make our money entirely from tips for our stage shows. Yet, in this scenario, the biggest earners aren't necessarily the most conventionally beautiful, and the most provocative stage show isn't always the most explicit or accomplished.

The pound-in-the-pot system used in many strip pubs means each customer doles out £1 ($1.50) to each of us before we go on stage. Once the girl ahead of you on the rota takes the stage, you have until the end of her performance to collect your tips. You move through the crowd, trying to remember who you have and haven't collected from, requesting your money with varying degrees of politeness, smiling with varying degrees of sincerity, trying to make the whole procedure frictionless. On a quiet daytime shift there's no rush, and you might find yourself dancing nude on stage for a few quid. But on busy nights there's more urgency. Most customers know the score and contribute happily, some are gracious and put in a note, but there's always the odd one who quibbles over parting with their pound. They trot out a host of well-trodden reasons, either unaware or unconcerned about how badly this reflects on them, or how limp with hatred you feel towards them. I don't have change.

I'm not going to watch you. I paid the last girl so why do I have to pay again? Sometimes they try to toss in a lesser coin, but your ear is finely tuned to distinguish between the clink of a pound versus a copper, even above the din. You can either call over the bouncer to mediate your request (and it's remarkable how quickly they manage to find the correct change when you're flanked by a pair of burly doormen), or you can cut your losses and move on ... because while you're quibbling with one cheap arsehole for a pound you could be collecting a great deal more from the group of pleasant, gracious customers next to him.

While horror stories of dancers humiliating themselves on stage become folklore – the forgotten string of a tampon, a fleck of remaining toilet paper illuminated in the UV light, a failed pole trick, a faulty suspender belt – many of us get a thrill from being up there. It can feel totally empowering or truly mortifying, and anywhere in between.

Trixie

HARMONY

It was a good night – I was making money. When you're on a roll and you're making money, you start feeling *more* confident and sexy, and then you make even more money. It was packed, a full house, so when I was on stage there were no seats left and people were standing at the back leaning against the walls. I really enjoyed that aspect of Friday, Saturday nights. It was always a bit hectic and you wouldn't be on stage very often, but then when you were it was really fun because you had a proper audience. I was probably dancing to something like Led Zeppelin's 'Ramble On' – a song that has those points where the bass drops and you can do big spins on the pole and the audience goes, Wow. And you're just in that zone on stage where you're just like, *I'm so fucking hot.*

I remember being on stage and just kind of being in my element. I remember seeing him, this guy. He was cute – cute in the context of the club, not in the context of the outside world. He was hot for strip-club-punter standards. Generally, 90 per cent of the guys that go to ▮▮▮▮▮▮▮ are not attractive, so if there's anyone that comes in that's slightly good looking then they just shine. We've all been there, where maybe you've done, like, four or five shifts and you've had no contact with the outside world, so you just kind of forget that there's normal attractive guys out there. And then someone with like, a bit of stubble comes into the club, and you're like, *Oh, he's really hot!*

He was like a fish out of water in there. He was a bit in awe and, I don't know, I guess I really got off on that because I felt really confident and powerful. It was my territory. I just made a beeline for him. We had a few dances, I was quite drunk. It was getting towards the end of the night, people were slowly leaving, and I was just a bit buzzy from the whole evening so I suggested we go somewhere for a drink afterwards. I remember him being like, Really? Like he couldn't believe this was really happening, that I might actually want him. I really got off on that.

We left the club and went to Shoreditch House. We got some drinks and we were up by the pool at the top where you can look out over London. It was a warm summer night and I remember vividly being on that balcony with him and realising that he didn't know my real name, like, *Wait, he still thinks my name is Harmony?!* That added to the experience of fantasy and role-play. What turned me on was that I was aware of how much power I had in the situation. For him, it was a total fantasy and I was so *up there*. So we were up on the top floor bar, and I can't remember who said it, but I think it was probably me who was just like, Should we go back to your house?

The whole lead-up to the sex was just so good because he could not believe his luck. We went to his flat in Hoxton – I think he must have been sharing, you know, flatmates and stuff, so we just went straight up the stairs to his attic bedroom. He had washing hanging out on one of those white metal racks that go over the radiator. It was a really neat and boring room. He wasn't like a big macho man, he was quite slim and pale skinned, and had quite weedy arms. I've had one-night stands with guys where I've just been like, Oh, your body is just so beautiful. You know, like an Adonis, like a god. He was not that at all. He was the opposite of that, which is quite funny. Because that one night I remember just having the most amazing sex with this guy, this weird little guy in this dull room.

I've slept with a lot of guys but I've never had that experience before, of that unbelievable anticipation where they're just bubbling over. His chest was touching mine and his body was actually shaking. I just thought that was like the biggest turn-on. And then we started taking each other's clothes off and I guess I was in character the whole time. That performance of the sex kitten on stage just kind of carried on, and I could be that same person, and move in that same way that I was in the club because, as far as he was concerned, that's who I was.

I remember fucking him and not feeling a hint of having to impress him. Normally, when you're going on a date with someone there's a sense of pressure that you want them to like you. But, with

WANTING YOU TO WANT ME

this guy, there was none of that because I'd started from *up there*, so I didn't have to censor myself in any way. I had no inhibitions or self-consciousness about how I looked to him. Basically, I could just use him to get me off.

I had so many orgasms, definitely the most orgasms I've ever had with a one-night stand. I was basically wanking myself off while we were having sex. And that was okay, I was allowed to do that. I kind of lost myself a little bit, I guess, I just completely let go. I think a lot of the time when you've had sex with guys that you've just met, or one-night stands or whatever, there's always a kind of element of keeping up appearances. But, you know, this time I could fully let go because this wasn't me, this was Harmony. So it kind of gave me permission to be that person and act that way. It was kind of a continuation of the role play that happens in a strip club. I wasn't thinking about seeing this guy again tomorrow, or what did this mean, or how does he see me? I was just thinking about pleasure, I guess. And that was it.

It's the same as what I was saying about being at the club: the more money you earn, the more confident and sexy you become, and it creates this positive cycle. It's the same thing when you're in bed with a guy. It's like, the more I let go and just did what I wanted with him in bed, the more of a turn-on that was for him, so it gathers momentum. And, I guess the thing is, I wasn't concerned with his experience, I just got off on the power. I got off on the fact that I was this goddess in his eyes, and I just ran with it. And then beyond that, I was quite selfish. You know, he's in my presence, so he's going to be having an amazing time, I didn't have to worry about him, know what I mean?

I've had periods of being incredibly promiscuous and having loads of one-night stands, but it's just different when it starts in that club, in that world. It just means that the energy is different. It was a total fantasy for him. So we had this amazing night, but it didn't last beyond that one night. Even when we'd woken up the next morning the spell had been broken.

Venus

Bex

POPPY

When I started I was so young. I mean, I looked like a child, so my ideal customer was any guy who looked like a paedo. I was 18 but I probably looked about 15 and I had no tits. I've had my tits done since then, and now I have tattoos, so I guess I can't really play that part anymore. But I wish I'd had the game then that I have now, 'cause I would've fucking rinsed it, I would've made so much money.

My first stage show was ... I didn't know anything about stripping. I was wearing a bowler hat. I may as well have had a cane. So awful! I was doing high kicks with my hat. My mum always took me to dance classes when I was younger, so all I had in terms of dance technique was jazz, tap and musical theatre. So I really gave it some theatre on stage. And I think a lot of people must have been laughing at me. I thought I was great; you know like you do when you're 18. But when I think back to my initial stage show – in fact, my stage shows in the first couple of years – I mean, they must have been awful. They must have been so funny to watch, proper comedy gold. I remember the audition song because it was always the same for everyone, it was that, you know, *No diggity, I like the way you work it*. So there I was doing the hat thing and the high kicks to 'No Diggity'.

I had a guy at ▬▬▬ – I was 18 at the time, so any money was big money to me – it was the easiest £50 ($70) I ever made. He told me he was a vampire and he had loads of rings and medallions on, he looked more like a vampire slayer if anything. He drank his bottle of beer, gave it to me and said, Fill it up with piss and I will drink it all and give you £50. So I went straight to the bathroom, I filled it up and then I watched him stare into my eyes and glug it down – then he gave me the £50 and I was like, *Sweet*. Easiest £50 I've ever made. The reason he told me he was a vampire was that he liked menstrual blood, so he asked me if I was on my period and if he could have my tampon, but I wasn't on. I love weird people like that.

Poppy

One of my favourite clients used to come in on a Wednesday daytime. Do you remember Mr. Magoo? Fred, the really old guy? He had big glasses and he was just proper filth. He was really old, like maybe nearly in his nineties. He'd come in every Wednesday and spend his pension money. He never gave me loads, but I will always remember him because he was so consistent. Every Wednesday. And all he wanted to do was, basically, you know that little private room? The one that was a singular private booth? He would sit at the end and I'd just lie on the floor with my legs spread doing my Kegels, making my pussy move. And I'd do that for maybe three songs and I'd get £60 ($80) out of it, then he'd always offer me a little mint. At the end, he'd be like, Do you want a Mento? As a character, I'll just always remember him, even though I never made loads of money out of him.

∴

I always used to use my own name at work. And the reason I always used it was because I was always myself at work, which actually was a really bad idea and I only came to realise that as I got older. So I created Poppy. It's really good to have a persona at work because you can kind of slip in and out of it, and when you're talking to people you don't get as offended if they don't like you, or if they don't want you, because they're not talking to you, they're talking to Poppy, the alter ego.

Oh my God, I wear the trashiest shit as Poppy. Poppy is more overtly sexual than I am. I've kind of built this whole new character that's a bit porn star-y, I guess. Poppy will always lead with sexually charged questions whereas I would never talk to someone like that. Poppy's just a bit of a slut, really. I am too, in my own right! But Poppy is much more overt, very over the top. When I started at ▬▬▬▬▬ I wasn't in the mindset of Poppy. I wasn't quite into this character that I've built now. My stripper persona that I have now is strong, but she wasn't strong before.

About three years ago I decided to be a career stripper, and I was like, *I'm gonna rinse this*. My game, I guess, is just the way that I interact with clients now; the way that I make money. I like to have quite a hard hustle now, whereas I never had that before. Before it would be like, *Well, I'll just see what happens!* And that was really cool and I had so much fun doing that because you'd get really nicely surprised every now and again with a great night. But then, when I went to Miami, I started living between there and London, going back and forth a lot and working over there in this ridiculous club called ███████. It's a 24-hour strip-club-cum-nightclub where you've got people like Drake performing and you've got big DJs and it is insane. There's rooms that are £1,500 ($2,000) an hour, it's a crazy place. I think I just got the bug there, because all the girls were proper hustlers and I thought, *Well, to keep up with them I need to really get on it and I need to be a hustler.* And that's where I kind of started, about three years ago. I was like, *I'm gonna make a career out of this, there's so much money to be made.* One night I made five grand and I was like, *This is sick!* And then the next night I went in and I made three grand. So I was just, like, propelled to be this hustler. Now I've bought my flat, I feel a bit more chill and I don't feel as much like I want to put that much energy into it. But in America, definitely, there's fucking money to be made in America so, if you're on it, you can make a lot.

In America I'll wear proper trash: neon string bikinis, anything with sparkles on it, anything over the top, anything that glows in the dark, I'm down for that. I always used to look at strippers when I was younger and think, *Why do they wear these awful outfits? They're so disgusting.* But, actually, I don't know if it's just like moths to a flame or something, but it really works! And I've noticed that the more glow-in-the-dark and the more sparkly I am in clubs, like in Vegas and Miami, the more attraction there is. If I just wear black, pretty lingerie – which I would choose to wear as myself – I would just go unnoticed in half of the clubs that I've worked at in America. So I now understand why stripper outfits are really trashy and neon and sparkly. I thought they were disgusting before but now I'm like, *No, it works! It makes you money!* So I would say I'm probably the trashiest dancer at ████████████, there's no other girls that dress like me here.

· ·
·

I do actually think that a lot of men who walk into a strip club, they walk in there for a reason – they want to be sexually charged. That's what they're looking for, right? So the more skin you have on show, the sluttier you look – it does work. There's very few men that are gonna go for a more demure look. Or maybe they've got an image in their head of the girl they want already so it doesn't matter what you're wearing or who you are, if you're not that, then you're not going to do it for them. But I have noticed, since changing up my look and being a bit trashier and more provocative, I appeal to the masses as opposed to a small group of people. Before, I think I was more appealing to the person who wanted to sit down and talk about interesting things and actually wanted to avoid the topic of sex altogether; the sort of guy who'd be like, No, just keep your clothes on. We all love those customers, but they're few and far between. So if I get those customers, great – but they're probably not gonna want me now. I'm okay with that because I'm there to do a job, right? And to make money, not really to be too specific.

I have some friends, like Chloe, she's really specific. She only appeals to a certain kind of customer, but when she does get them they're really good. So I don't know, maybe it is worthwhile for some people. But I just feel like I don't want to put too much of myself or my soul into it anymore. I'd rather just be this character, go into work, be disgusting, and not feel like I have to take on any of the baggage, or the shit, or the heavy energy. Then I literally just rid myself of it when I walk out the door.

This all makes me sound like I hate my job. I don't, I really like it. I just think you've gotta be so protective of yourself when you do this job, because it can really have a negative effect on you if you don't do it in the right way. That's something I wish someone would have told me from the beginning: don't be yourself too much, because that's a lot that you're giving to people. You're giving away so much of your own energy if you just walk into a club and are one hundred per cent yourself, and you have to be this really open and honest and fun person, you know that's really difficult if you are playing yourself. So it makes it so much easier being a character.

My hustle was to lead with something sexual straight away. I really enjoy the dirty talk, I always lead with it because I just feel you can get into character with it, you can just say whatever you want. If *I* was talking dirty to someone I'd be rubbish, but Poppy can talk dirty to people. It's weird 'cause I don't really even do it with boyfriends, but I can do it with customers.

So I'll go up to a guy and the first thing that I'll get them to do is sit down and get comfy. I'll always be touching my tits or, like, touching my mouth, or making sex eyes at them. And my line at the moment is, I've got a really, really, really tiny pussy. And I just keep saying it to people and I feel like it just engages them straight away in the sex chat, and I'll just talk about sex very overtly. Recently, I fucked my friend's husband, because she wanted me to, and she was there too and she filmed it. And that was just totally a private thing in my life, but I'm bringing it into Poppy's life now as well, and I'm sometimes leading with that story. Or sexual things that I've done or a friend has done, I'll make it out like it's me. So, yeah, I always lead with the sex. I always try to make them think that it's their idea, that they want to spend money on me and take me upstairs to the VIP room. I always tell them that they can touch me and that they can do things that they probably can't, things I would probably put them in their place for. Even if I can't get a VIP out of someone, I will try to get whatever out of them, which is kind of horrible, but ... even if it's just a dance. I'll always sell two dances at a time, like, I'll never sell one unless it's fucking dead and I'm feeling desperate. Always up-sell. It's harder here in England. Here, sometimes there's no one in the clubs so you don't even have the ability to hustle. Or people are literally like, I've got £25 ($35). And I'm like, *For fuck's sake.*

Here it does feel very different to working in America, but I still lead with the overtly sexual stuff, which just gets people. And also there's another technique which is really cool ... Once you've got a guy in the VIP and you wanna keep him there longer, you can start talking about his sexual fantasies, and, basically, you play the either-or game. So, you'd say to them, In your sexual fantasy are you inside or are you outside? And then they say, Oh, we'd be inside. Then I'd say, Are you with one person? Or are you with more than one person? Oh, well, I'm with two girls. Okay, so you're inside with two girls ... And then you repeat it back to them and you have this whole setup in their head and they've created it, but you've kind of given them these really simple options. Also, I always try to say things like, I'm sorry if I'm wasting your time, I can always go and speak to someone else ... Always give them the idea that you're gonna leave them, because that's the key issue that most men have, which is fear of abandonment. So always dangle the carrot in front of their face, like, Oh, I could leave you and talk to someone else. And then normally they're like, No, no, stay here.

Embedded commands are also really good. An embedded command is like, Pay me. Or like, Be generous. Stuff like that. And you can slip that into normal conversation. You have to say it in a certain way as well, with the tone of your voice. So you have to say it like, I'd really like it if you could *pay* me attention. I've used mimicking for a long time, too. Basically, if someone has a certain tone, if they naturally speak at a certain register, you try to do the same. Or if they say certain words slightly differently you try to do that too. Or even body language. If someone is sitting in front of you in the bar and they have one elbow up, I'll put one elbow up. If someone has an accent – I do it naturally as well – I start to take on their accent. And then there's anchors, which means that every time you say something positive to someone, you touch them on their right arm, or you stroke the inside of their wrist, or you touch your boob, something like that. It's positive reinforcement and they connect that together, subconsciously.

· ·
·

Yeah, I have a few regulars. One of them is a regular from ███████, his name's Ian. He's a fucking pain in the arse, but I would say that he paid for most of my year last year. He would come in weekly and always spend over a grand, and if I went to dinner with him he'd give me a grand. When I was in America, if I was like, Oh, I need some money in my bank account! He would send me money. But with that comes this whole thing that I have to call him and I have to text him and I speak to him more than I speak to some of my family members, so it's a lot. And he actually knows where I fucking live as well, which always creeps me out because he used to live on this street. He bought me this phone and he pays for the bill. He's got like this sort of hold over me in a sense. So I have to be really careful with that dynamic, too, because I don't want it to ever get weird.

It's been just over a year now. He knows the date that we met. I don't. He's quite a boring guy and I think that he likes girls that are a little bit like party girls, basically, which, when I met him I really was. I was like in the depths of party land. It would be seven in the morning at ▮▮▮▮▮▮▮ and I'd be doing cartwheels while he's sort of laughing at me. So he is that person who likes that high-energy sort of sit-down. I think that's why he likes it, 'cause he's quite a boring person himself. He comes from quite a fair amount of money. And he's a little guy, people call him Small Hands because he's got the tiniest hands you've ever seen on a guy. They are weirdly small, like, really weirdly small. He's told me basically that he's in love with me, so I'm gonna keep going on with that.

I do dance for him, but not that much. He's besotted with me and more, like, in love with me. I don't think he's an overly sexual man. He's more like ... when I dance for him he'll stare into my eyes, that kind of guy. Which I'm like, *Bleugh!* But, no, it's fine, it works for me. Because a whole evening of getting touched up could be a bit much. I think if he was really quite a sexual person it would annoy me and I would have to cut it short quickly because there's only so long that I can deal with someone trying to grab my pussy. So it's kind of nice actually that he's not like that but, yeah, he is a bit of a drip. He calls me his girlfriend. He basically said to his niece the other day, Oh, my girlfriend might come out for lunch with us. And he reported this back to me and I was like, *Okay, so he thinks we're in a relationship.* I don't know whether he does or whether he's playing the game too, because he's been playing the stripper game and the stripper scene for a long time, for like 10 years.

When customers leave the club, they'll be rushing afterwards. It's kind of like that feeling you get if you're having an affair or if you're dating someone that you shouldn't be, and after you've left you're still rushing off the high of, like, what just happened!? So I think that they probably enjoy that aftermath as well because it's like a drug.

I do fancy customers sometimes. I went out with my ex-boy-friend for five years and he was a customer. I met him in █████████ and I didn't necessarily fancy him, I was just having a fucking mental breakdown and I felt like he was really gonna solve all my issues because he just seemed really caring and he had a lot of money. And, actually, there was also a guy in Vegas who was fucking beautiful. He's a French-Canadian singer, and he'd come in for a bachelor party to this club in Vegas and I was just really horny and needed to fuck someone. I did a few dances with him, made a bit of money out of him, and then I was like, Anyway, can I have your number? I wanna fuck you. He was really young; he was only 26 but he was really beautiful and really sweet. He was like, What, tonight?! And I was like, No, because you're shit-faced and I don't want to fuck a drunk guy. So I met up with him the next day. I went to his hotel room, fucked him, ordered room service and left.

They still have to do something for me in the club, though. They still have to give me money because it's a turn off if they say no. I met this guy last week who was fucking hot. He came into █████████ and I was like, *Oh my God, he looks like Tom Hardy.* He was so hot, I would have fucked the shit out of him. So I was hoping he was gonna take me upstairs and, even if we only do like half an hour or an hour in VIP, I don't care, I would definitely give him my number and meet up with him. Anyway, it gets to it and he's like, Oh, I'm not gonna pay because I can't really afford it. I'll only come if my boss can pay. I was like, *Do you know how much of a turn off that is right now? Like, my pussy just dried up.* And then we all went up as a group and his boss was gonna pay and then the card got declined, and I was like, *Ugh, that's just gross.* It's not like they have to pay me loads of money, but it's just that whole thing of, like, you're paying me and then I'm gonna give you sex later just because I want to! There's this whole story it's got to follow, and if it doesn't follow that, then no. And I kind of wish sometimes that guys would know that, because if only you knew I would fuck you – I one hundred per cent will! But I just want you to do this one thing for me in the club, because it's part of the fucking story. Stupid men.

It's getting to my 10 years, but I honestly feel like I've got another 10 years in me – as long as I can be sober. Everything balances on my sobriety. Because I can really easily go off the rails, so as long as I keep that then I think I could definitely do it longer. It's so much more than just a job, it's a lifestyle, it's a personality, it's everything, and it's where you meet most of your really good friends as well. So the connection that I guess we have to stripping … it's not just a job, it's not like someone's office job, it's so much more than that. I don't see how you could ever be separate from it.

Poppy

Poppy

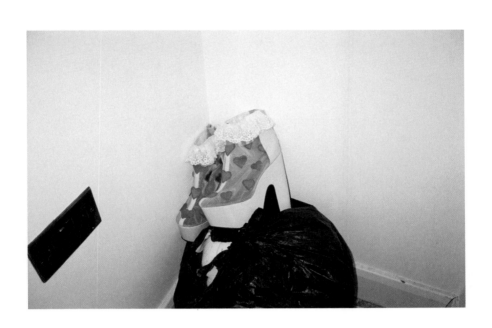

Poppy

CHIQUI

I remember when I was like 17 there was this programme on TV called *Crónicas Marcianas*, which means Chronicles from Mars. And it was this variety talk show that had all these really freaky people. They had this really camp Venezuelan guy, and this witch that used to predict the future really badly … and then they had this stripper called Chiqui Martí. That was the first time I saw a proper pole show, and she was absolutely amazing. She was a bit goth-looking and had this beautiful red hair. At the end when she took her pants off, she would like, cover herself somehow. I found it so beautiful what she did, I thought it was such an art. So when I went for an audition and I needed to pick a stage name, she was the first person that came to mind, because I thought she was so beautiful and I really enjoyed watching her.

I always had this flamboyance because, again, I do come from a culture that is very colourful and happy and I had this kind of Amazonian idea of women. I remember on Latin American TV in Venezuela, you had these super fucking good-looking women wearing tiny G-strings, dancing. So to me it was not a huge, shocking thing to do that. But then obviously, you also have the moralistic issue of religion and stuff … so it's funny because you come from a culture that somehow really puts women on this kind of goddess-like, sexual pedestal wearing these tiny bikinis, but at the same time they really slap you with the whole religious morality thing. So I was very influenced by all of that. My first audition I wore a Union Jack–sequinned bikini with beads all over the place and I danced to 'Livin' La Vida Loca' by Ricky Martin. I've refined my act over the years, but the essence is the same.

∵

WANTING YOU TO WANT ME

The first place I danced was ████████████ in Shoreditch. For me, the pub scene in London suited me better than the big clubs. It was not the most glamorous place on earth, it's far from that, but that kind of dodgy environment somehow suited me better than a big club with leopard-print carpet and a hundred girls on a shift. So yeah, I started there and the money was okay actually, back in the day. This was in 2003. Also, let's remember that I come from South America, so whatever money I was making, to me it was a lot. I was coming from working in hospitality, doing bar work and stuff. So when I made money at ████████████, maybe compared to the big clubs it was nothing, but for me it was a lot.

Even though the place was horrendous, it's the only place where I really truly found a huge variety of dancers. You had big ladies, Black women, Asian girls, you even had this Bangladeshi dancer, too. So now when I look back at it, I regard it with love and compassion because of how fucking cool it was to have such a variety of girls. It's actually one of the most diverse strip clubs I ever worked at. In fact, there was this dancer who was maybe, like, 70 years old, Mona. She was great. And I haven't seen anything like it since then. After that it became pretty white and a lot of this doll-ish kind of look.

There were private dances, but it was really all about the table dances. You would dance on an actual table that had a pole in the middle. The guys were sitting down, and if you were kneeling then your pussy would be right at eye level. So you were literally a goddess on a pedestal. I loved it. I've never seen anything like it anywhere else. At the other places I worked, it was normal lap dancing. But this idea of being on top of a table and the guys looking up at you, I thought that was pretty cool.

I used to love this one place called ████████████, where you'd only have two girls on a shift. It was really funny 'cause you had to put a pound in the jukebox and that would give you five songs. There was no stage so you just got naked around the pub, and every 15 minutes you and the other girl would take turns. The guys were just there having a pint, and you'd just go around to each table, show your tits, then you go to the next table and show your butthole, and then you could even go on the pool table. These guys are playing pool, and you were like, Oh, sorry guys, I'm just going to show you my lady bits. And they'd be like, Oh no, just jump in. So I'd jump on the pool table and open my legs, touch myself, and get off the pool table. You would just walk around this pub slowly taking your clothes off, it was fucking hilarious. Like, I just love how random and how English that was, like a proper Benny Hill sort of thing.

..
.

My most favourite place that I ever worked, in the heyday, was ████ ██████████, for sure. Because the vibe was great among the girls, there was a sort of family atmosphere there. The shows were fucking amazing, *really* good dancers, money was good. It was just really, really fun. From the outside it looked like a very traditional English pub. On the inside, there was this tiny stage in the corner with a pole on it. And behind the stage, there was a screen that showed football and boxing, and guys could get lunch there. This place will open from twelve thirty in the afternoon till like one in the morning. So guys, back in the day, would come from the City and were able to have their lunch break there. These guys would come in and eat their jacket potato with a little bit of salad right at the front of the stage, with the football playing on the background. You were fully naked with your crotch right in this guy's face while he's eating his potato with beans and cheese, and somebody scoring a fucking goal on this screen behind you.

I think the thing that really made that club stand out is that it was run by two East End ladies, you know, like proper East End women. It was a mum and a daughter, which I think somehow made it better. I mean, I don't want to say that female managers are better 'cause I've met some horrible female managers, but this particular duo was charismatic in a very kind of East London way. They had really good taste in dancers, I think that all of the dancers there were spectacular in their own way. Like, the best pole shows, charisma, stage personas, just the best strippers as a whole were at ████████ ██████. They really focused on giving guys a good show. And also, I think it was quite diverse in body shapes and stuff, which was really nice to see too. It's located right at the edge of the City, so sometimes you have your bankers, but sometimes you'll have your construction workers, or guys that were partying the whole weekend in Shoreditch – 'cause back in the day Shoreditch had wild nightlife. You'd have guys that hadn't slept for like three days, and then they come to the ███████████ on a Sunday lunch. We used to have a Sunday lunch shift which we called the Sunday service. So you'd have the hipsters and the artists, but also the market traders, people working on Petticoat Lane who would pop in for a beer. So it was such a cool and interesting crowd. I think one of my favourite crowds was the Friday lunch shift because you have all the construction workers that would usually be super generous, and then you'll have your City boys, too, so it was fun. I loved how eclectic the crowd was, always super down to earth and, like, very British.

My favourite time working there was before they started doing private dances, because we could really focus on our stage shows. The talent and the amount of great performance at the ██████ ████████ really shined during those days because that was how you made your money. If you'd put on a good stage show then you had more tips and, also, in between the shows you could talk to guys just because you wanted to and it was like, chill. Later it became all about the hustle for private dances. Back in the day, it was five girls on a shift, each of us would do five stage shows, and before each stage show we'd come around with a little pint glass and we'd go like, Can I get a pound please for my show? Can I get some tips from my show? And then they'd put a coin in there, or sometimes if you're lucky you get some notes. Then the DJ would call you, Please welcome to the stage, the lovely Chiqui! Then you dance one song on stage and that was it.

To be honest, I play the Latina card, you know. 'Cause guys are quite basic, and I will play reggaeton and like super Latin music on stage 'cause that will really make me stand out. Even though it's not particularly what I would normally listen to, sometimes in a strip club you really have to stand out, especially if there's loads of girls, so I will totally play the role of the extra Latina one. I will be the token Latina, I'll just fucking have that. And that works at any age.

My selling point was my dancing, you know, like I was one of the best dancers and I'm not saying this in an arrogant way, but I'm engaging on the stage, you know? But then it became more about private dances and the number of girls increased. So now you could only do three stage shows a night and you had to hustle guys in between for private dances, which were £10 ($14) at lunchtime and £20 ($28) in the evening. Obviously we're all beautiful, we're all strippers, but some girls have that kind of beauty that guys really just fall for easily. And if you had two of those girls on your shift, you were completely fucked. You have the girl with massive boobs and the blonde hair and you're like, *Oh, fuck*. You don't wanna feel like it's your fault, but it does just mess with your self-esteem.

When it was just stage shows, you didn't have the pressure to only be sexy or beautiful or naïve; but when you're selling private dances, there's only so much you can do without freaking men out. Back in the day, I had complete open creativity, 'cause I was like, *Well, they have to pay a fucking pound anyway, so I can do whatever the fuck I want*. For one of my most favourite shows I dressed up as a sailor, and I made all of the guys in the audience sing 'In The Navy' by the Village People while I was shaking my nipple tassels. I also had this show where I was Dorothy from *The Wizard of Oz*, and I had this battery-operated dog that humped my leg, and everybody was just laughing their heads off. So yeah, it was a lot of fun, fun times there for sure. It was really nice to have that space to be creative, and guys really responded to it. In fact, I was booked pretty much every Friday, which was a good shift to have. But after the private dances started I noticed that they went for the more traditional beauty, you know, like sexy but not too intelligent or sassy. More of the plain sort of thing. And I kind of struggled with that. I found that quite hard to deal with. I mean, I definitely adapted, but I found it a bit harder because I felt I had to tone it down a bit just because you want to make money, and, you know, if you're wearing a freaking clown costume not many guys get a hard-on. Well, very specific guys get a hard-on, but they weren't there.

I also felt there was tension there, even though we all got along really well and it was this beautiful atmosphere, at the end of day you are competing with your friends. I always found that a little bit weird because you do love them, but at the same time you feel a bit like … *Shit, I also need to make money.* Also, as strong as you want to be, your self-esteem really suffers when you see certain people having like maybe 10 private dances in a shift, and you're there having only three, thinking, *Fuck! What is wrong with me? I'm ugly.* I felt like it was really affecting my self-esteem sometimes. Even though it's completely stupid, like you know you shouldn't put your value in that shit, but you do.

• •
•

Marcus has been coming to see me dance for like 13 years now. In fact, since I moved to Berlin he has come to visit three times. So yeah, we're still in touch, we message each other all the time. I've had a couple of others but the one that's lasted the longest has been Marcus for sure. He's definitely my longest relationship. I think he also has another girl that he sees sometimes from Czech Republic, and we physically look similar, but he's a lovely guy. I think with him the boundaries are very clear. He understands what our relationship is. It's a sexy friendship. However, we do also feel a lot of love for each other. Like, I respect him a lot and he respects me. It's a sexual friendship and it's a beautiful friendship, and I think me and Marcus are going to be friends for a very long time.

Funnily enough, throughout this pandemic, I have found that the guys who have been my customers have been a lot more caring and giving than guys I have fucked for free. Like, customers have been messaging me often, Chiqui, are you okay? Or sometimes they send me a little PayPal thing for wine or something. Marcus has helped me pay my rent a couple of times throughout this pandemic, which is super sweet. So it's funny because people think that we don't develop feelings for these guys, but in my particular case, I did.

I think when people judge the stripper-customer relationship, it comes from a place of privilege. Because what people forget is a lot of my customers are not the best-looking guys. You know, like they're a bit fat or maybe they work ridiculous hours so their social skills aren't really up to scratch. We live in a society that values looks, money and success so much. And if you don't have that, it's like you're not valid. And, actually, Marcus is a very sensual person; when you look at him you wouldn't necessarily be attracted to him, but then you talk to him and he's a lovely guy. We value looks so much that people forget, like, what about the rest? What about the ones that don't have any of these attributes, are we going to neglect them completely? To be honest, every time I have danced for Marcus, I had the best time, and he's always asking me, Are you okay? Is everything alright?

When I was working full time, the last thing I wanted to do was date anyone. I was so exhausted from having this chat, Where are you from? How old are you? How long have you been here? You have those conversations 10 times a night in a club, so when you have time off you're emotionally exhausted. Also, you're being deeply performative so much, it sometimes becomes blurry when you're actually acting and when you're not. You're being flirty and sassy and loving for six, nine hours a night. Now that I haven't been dancing for well more than a year with the whole pandemic, I finally had the energy, so I went out with a guy for seven months. But the thing is, you see them so clearly, you become a lot less patient with men. I even struggle to sleep in the same bed with a guy, you know. I fuck and then I need to go home.

Maybe it's also an age thing. I'm almost 40 now, so I guess your limits are a bit stricter but, yeah, it definitely makes you tell the good men from the bad men. I always say to guys what I do for a living straight away, and I feel like how they treat a marginalised group of women says a lot about them. I always say it pretty much on the first date. I'm like, This is what I do and it's not going to change, because it's such a big part of my life.

I look younger than my age, but I've never lied about it. Sometimes you get the ones that get really freaked out because they want the really young-looking girls, which I always found a bit creepy. But I've also found, for example, if there's a father and a son, the father will go with a younger stripper and the son will go with me. I think at some point I became a source of experience for younger guys. They feel really attracted to that. So I get the occasional 20-somethings because they see you as this goddess of knowledge. But sometimes with older guys, you know, the decent ones, they feel more comfortable having a dance with me than with someone who's 21.

I want to see more older women on stage. I want to start running workshops with women in their forties, fifties, sixties. Because I feel sexier than ever, you know, with all this wisdom and knowledge I have now. And I think it's really cool to start breaking boundaries about who's allowed to be sexy on stage. I'm like, *Fuck it. I'm gonna be sexy on stage forever.* And every time I see another woman with her tits out on stage, I'm like *Fucking good for you. Let's do it.*

What's the feeling of being on stage? I think to be honest, that's my happy place. Out of everything in life, my most favourite moments are when I'm on stage in front of a good crowd. More than sex, more than eating, more than travelling – and I love travelling, I love going to new countries – but not even that, no. Oh, I just want to be on the fucking stage. And I want people to be having it! There's nothing like it. That is the thing that makes me the happiest. More than anything, like even spaghetti Bolognese, which I fucking love. On the stage with a happy crowd is my most favourite place.

People are never going to get tired of sex and entertainment, especially after coronavirus. After the pandemic I think people are going to be hornier than ever.

Chiqui

BEX

I'd always danced from a young age. I've done ballet and performing and I kind of thought it was gonna be like that. So with the stage shows, strangely I was immediately pretty comfortable with it 'cause I was okay with my own body and I wasn't shitting myself about performing. I did not realise that I'd have to have a personality as well. I thought I was gonna turn up, look pretty and job done. And it turned out to be something altogether different. I was like a rabbit in the headlights at first because I was only 19 or 20 and really and truly didn't know who I was.

When I first started dancing I went to audition at ███████ ████ in London and I ate tuna and cucumber sandwiches with ████ ██████████ and his assistant in the afternoon. That was a surreal experience in and of itself. It was everything you'd expect. The red velvet and the leopard print, and █████, I think, was sat in a gold throne.

For my audition, I ended up doing a stage dance to George Michael, 'Jesus to a Child'. I was having to dance really slowly, and I've ended up always dancing slowly actually, I sort of found my style at my audition and kept it. And then I sat down and they were like, Oh they'd love you in Paris, because you're so sort of elegant and very petite, I think you'd do really well in Paris. They'll love you over there. So I just kind of went along with it. I was that kind of character. And then they booked me a Eurostar ticket.

Peter had taken a real shine to me. I was his type, apparently. I was very young, very slim, and he ended up letting me live in his apartment in Paris on the Champs-Élysées when he wasn't there. I dunno, I feel like he was trying to make me his girlfriend. So, at this point I'm 21 years old, I've got the keys to a multi-million-pound flat on the Champs-Élysées, I've got money being thrown at me, like, quicker than I can count it and I just fucking lived it up like you wouldn't believe. I was fucking off to Saint-Tropez at weekends, I was shagging

Bex

a guy who was a striker of – I won't tell you what football club – a very famous football club, and I just really, really lived it up.

The club in Paris, before it was a strip club it was a very classy bar and restaurant. So it had that kind of charm and they hadn't made it tacky or anything like that. It actually had a bit of class. A lot of clubs now in London, they don't know what they're trying to emulate, but I think they're influenced by this boutique hotel strip club look. But back in fucking 2006, that's how this club in Paris actually looked. That's how it authentically was. All the girls were wearing the most beautiful lingerie, it was so glamorous. They'd only opened up three strip clubs in Paris at this point and the French, the way they were seeing it was very much like a delicacy, you know, it was more like being considered being a Moulin Rouge dancer or at Crazy Horse.

The men would come in dressed in beautiful suits and at the tables, everyone drank Dom Pérignon. But not in the way that people in clubs in London drink Dom Pérignon, like with sparklers and stuff, there were no fucking sparklers coming out. It was just quiet wealth, like stealth wealth. Everyone was unbelievably thin, that's the one thing I would say about the girls. It was very French in that respect. We were all size six to eight. And then they'd call you to a table and you'd sit down. I didn't really speak French but it didn't matter. You just kind of would sit there and they'd hand you a wodge of these tickets, which could be exchanged at the end of the night for cash. It was so beautiful. I don't think it was a typical strip club experience. I think it's something that they're trying to copy now. But I don't think you'll ever see that again, because a lot of that was paid for on company cards. Which explains why people were so relaxed about spending that amount of money.

Going back to fucking Leicester after that was rather a shock to the system, I fucking hated it. I came back because I had to finish my course, I was doing a law degree. But I hated studying law. From the second I walked back in the door, all I wanted to do was run around, get my kit off and you know, just fucking live it up. I didn't want to do no essays and shit. I did actually get my law degree, but it really was a mad experience and then after that I just carried on dancing. I was going between London, New York and Paris for the next 10 years of my life.

I might be biased 'cause I'm working there at the moment, but my favourite UK club is actually ███████ in Soho, London. It's got character. I like that I can do what I want there. It's my favourite club and I've worked in some very glamorous establishments.

When you walk in the main door there's the bar on the left-hand side and there's neon lights – it's very neon-trash – and there's about two or three hundred bottles that people have brought back from all over the world when they've been away, you know those horrible bottles of booze that get left on a shelf after a Christmas party and not drank for three years. There's a lot of that hanging around. And then there's a lot of photos printed out and made into a collage on the walls – from before we had digital photos, all of the girls. I don't know if they realised they were going to be on the wall, but some of them have got their legs spread and, you know, there's full-frontal pornographic images and, of course, all the customers are in it too and a lot of them have got moustaches. Quite often you get customers coming in and they say, I'm on the wall! And they'll go off and find themselves and there they are with their head between someone's legs.

They recently put a new carpet in which was like a big event, a really big event. I think they thought they were quite flash when they got the new carpet. And then you go downstairs, quite steep stairs that every other night someone falls down, and it's usually always a customer. There you have the main stage where, bizarrely, there's a massive fake bone, a sort of huge prop bone that the girls sit on. The customer seats are like cinema seats – I think they must've been bought second-hand off a cinema that went out of business – rows and rows of cinema seats with little drink holders that have been there for 30 years. And then there are mirrors all along one wall, and then around the rest of the walls, how would you describe it ... murals of naked girls. It's kind of styled to look like the Parthenon with these great big pillars, but with these bitches stood in front of the pillars naked. And some of the girls who are in these photos are still working there and time has not perhaps been that kind to them. They're immortalised at their peak on the wall, and you see them now, you know five or 10 more years at ███████ and, shall we just say, things have spread.

The private dance area is covered with mirrors so it's like a maze of mirrors. While you're doing the dance you can see about 25 reflections of your naked ass in the mirrors by the way that they're angled, and it's not really flattering lighting. It looks a bit like a haunted house, like a funhouse at the funfair, you know, when you go in the ghost train or something. And there's one little booth that I like to call the VIP because it's slightly more private than the others, but it's a bit like a corridor, actually. Um, and of course all the – I guess I shouldn't say – but all the girls know where the cameras are.

It's actually protected in Soho as a theatre, apparently. It's got some sort of special status so they can't change the usage. Downstairs where the stairs are, it's like a proper sort of theatre backstage, and there's these big double doors with a heart on it, a big cushion heart that leads to the stage – but it's so decrepit and the heart is all broken and peeling off, which I think is kind of an interesting metaphor. Upstairs there are two broken fridges, a big changing room and a little kitchen bit where there are various kitchen appliances that have died and not been taken out. And then there's the smoking area, which is absolutely covered in pigeon shit.

∴

I don't need to own a TV now or really read any gossip magazines or trash on the internet about celebrities. I mean, I've got all the drama going on on a daily basis, and it's better than any *The Only Way Is Essex, Made in Chelsea* or fucking *Footballers' Wives*. The club's got everything rolled into one. I very rarely get bored on a shift there. There are characters there who, in any other walk of life, would be referred to a doctor, whereas there they're hiding in plain sight. I don't think the interior has been changed since the 80s. I mean, it's been there since the 60s in Soho and a lot of the customers haven't changed in the last 30, 40 years. So they come in like these dinosaurs. Loads of really interesting characters. It's got some charm. It's not sanitised. In a lot of the clubs, they're trying to manufacture an atmosphere. There's also no house mum – a lot of clubs have a house mum, which, you know, kind of controls the girls.

Because the house fee is low, some people just don't seem that pressured into really making a lot of money. I swear to God, I honestly believe some of them just go there to hang out. They're just there to chill out in the afternoon, drink some booze. You know, they've got regulars who buy them some drinks, and give them 20 or 40 quid for a chat. You know, they've probably just about covered the bills with it. And some of the girls, well … whereas for instance, in Paris, the girls would all be size eight, and sort of looking like Agent Provocateur models, but at ███████, you'll have girls who are over-weight, you'll have a girl whose got her tongue split in two directions, you know, you've got a full plethora of types. There's not the same hierarchical thing going on. If you go to some of the big West End clubs, it's very much who's skinniest and prettiest and who's had the most plastic surgery. In ███████ it's just, there's none of that. I mean, it must have a hierarchy in itself, but if there is a hierarchy it's more like maybe who's been there longest, if anything.

I've been working a few day shifts recently and I see a lot of the auditions 'cause they're in the day, and how they run them is they get the other girls to watch the auditions and decide. So the managers don't pick, it's the girls on the day shift who decide who gets the job or not. So, if someone comes in and we just randomly get the feeling that they might be a bit of a twat, we'll say no, just on that basis. Yeah, they've got to fit in with the vibe and it's not just about being really hot, it's like how your personality was when you walked in the door, you know, everything like that. Sometimes the customers would go down and watch. We'd get a regular to go down and watch and then come back up and tell us if the girl was okay. And the customers love it because they love feeling important. It's part of the fun of the day shift, holding the auditions. It's just not run like any other strip club at all.

• •
•

I like the stage show because I quite like being in control, I'm a control freak and I know that the moment I go on stage – I've got you. I feel like the Pied Piper on that stage. I can play the game and you're going to do what I say. Do I take a moment before I go on stage? There's probably a split second where I kind of slightly switch my focus into a kind of hyper-bitch mode. I think every stripper's got their own stage persona. Some of them are cheekier and having a laugh, some do a lot of tricks, and mine is kind of bitchy, I think. So I go on the stage, which has got two poles, and the trick is to dance and make everyone think that you're dancing personally just for them but not let on that you're doing that to everybody else too. There's a way of dancing where you can sort of slide down the pole, giving someone eye contact and really drawing them into your focus and making them think that you're not looking at them because you want their money, but because you're genuinely attracted to them. They think they're having a moment with you, but then you can twirl around and do it to somebody else on the other side of the room without them realising it. The secret definitely is eye contact, one hundred per cent. I dance slowly because I think that's a better way to draw people in, because there's a lot to check out on a human body. And if you're constantly going round the poles really fast, you can't pick up the details, which is where it's really interesting.

I know instantly when I've gone on the stage who is thinking, *Oh! I like her.* You know, who's lifted their head up and whose ears have pricked up – or whose dick has pricked up, more like – to my presence. And then I will zone in on them. Because your stage show is your advertisement, you know ... it's not so much even a chance to sell your stuff, it's your chance to make a connection. And once you've got that connection established, then they will generally want to continue it to a private dance. I've been doing this job for years and I usually know when I can get money off someone at that stage. Also, if you pay attention to the girls doing the stage shows before you, you get to know who's got money in their pocket and who's just wasting your time.

. .
.

I think the main secret ingredient would be confidence. When I feel more confident, I make more money. That's the number one thing. You have to speak to so fucking many people, and that gives you a certain amount of power. It's not normal to strike up a conversation with any fucking random stranger, you know, and make a friendship. Another thing about the hustle is knowing your customer. Like, knowing which kind of customer is yours. 'Cause every girl's got their own type that likes them. Know who's likely to get along with you. For me, it's generally older men who like to engage in conversation. And, for me, one thing I've learned is just the ability to listen, really. And be able to talk on a wide, wide range of subjects. If you get someone talking about something they're passionate about, they will generally stay talking with you for ages. I hear a lot of girls going up and saying, Hey, how are you? What's your name? Where are you from? You know, like the standard small talk. You need to get the fuck away from small talk as soon as possible because the small talk is what they've heard off all the girls all night. You're almost better off going up and insulting someone and taking the piss out of them than doing small talk. Make people forget that they're in a strip club, as if they might be having a conversation down at their local pub or out on a date, and then you can talk over a wide range of subjects. It's like manufacturing a friendship with someone who you may not necessarily meet in your day-to-day life. You wouldn't believe how you can find common ground with almost anyone.

People have amazed me over the years with the stuff that they've come out with. When you really get a customer, that's when they start telling you really intimate details of their entire life. They'll sit and pay you all night because they feel like you're this person that they've connected with, that they're ready to open up with, and they'll pay you a lot for that when really they should be paying a good therapist. I'm really, really listening, not just waiting for my chance to speak, but really, really, really carefully trying to figure out who this person is and what they're saying to me. They're happy when they leave. I do genuinely end up liking a lot of my customers. I try to find something to like about people, but I think that's a good thing to do not just in strip clubs, but in life – try to find something you like about people.

∴

Why do men come to strip clubs? One reason is because everyone wants to feel desired. And even if they know that they're paying for it, the girls are so good at engineering that feeling. Whether they've paid upfront or paid afterwards, they've bought into that moment. And it's just to deal with that very, very basic human desire to feel wanted. Even if it is completely fake. Even if it's, *I want your money*, that's good enough, you know. *I want your cash* can feel the same as *I want you*. And that is powerful. The other reason is, like I said, the people who come in on the day shift are misfits. People who are just straight up lonely, who don't really have anywhere else to go where they feel a part of anything. And if they're at a club with lots of regulars, they feel like this is my local pub. It just happens to be a local pub with a lot of girls in it. If they went to their actual local pub, the other blokes would just take the piss out of them. The other reason is, you get men coming in who are in stages of emotional crisis, either their marriage is breaking down or they're losing their business or they're having mental health issues. And they are too proud to go and see a professional and somehow they end up coming into strip clubs and seeing sex workers of different sorts. Of course, you've also just got the standard people who are out there to have a laugh and a stag night or birthday party – lads. There's also a very small proportion of men who come in to try and play some sort of game with people. And yet another reason is to feel young again. A lot of men are coming in to feel young again.

What's the appeal of the VIP rooms? I guess it's about showing that you have money and feeling important because you've got it. Also, when you spend more money the girls get more excited around you. That's why they do it. To feel important, the same reason why people go first class on a 45-minute flight and stuff like that. I mean, you don't really need to, but it's even like that with private members clubs if you think about it, it's just a fucking club. Like, why are you paying thousands of pounds a year to go sit in some fucking place? I dunno, it's just some dumb shit that rich people do.

The power games are the reason why a lot of people are there. From my viewpoint, some nights I think, *Yeah, I'm in control of everything here.* And some nights I genuinely am. But there are other nights where I just feel like, *Hang on, it's not going my way.* And on those nights, you know, the power could have gone to another girl, it might have gone to the customer, it might've gone to the management – and that's the worst thing. A lot of the time the power is taken by the management and the staff on a power grab. So it fluctuates, it's never in one place, it's moving like water and finding its level. It's not a constant.

If I hadn't ever danced, I feel like I might still be under the illusion that men are in charge of stuff. But now I actually see them for the fraudsters they are. They don't know any more than us. I mean, we don't want to talk about the patriarchy, but if I hadn't danced, I'd still be buying into it. I wouldn't have seen through the illusion that somehow they're more important than we are, because now I've seen that … well, first of all, they're easy to manipulate. It's not that it's changed my opinion of guys, it's changed my opinion of myself in relation to them, you know? So I might've just been kind of a stereotypical 'good woman', get married, have two kids, behave herself, don't fuck too many people. And now I've seen you don't necessarily have to play by those rules. The other thing is, before I started dancing, I would see a man who was being very kind of alpha-y and sort of show-off-y as kind of intimidating and frightening. But now I just see the insecurity behind it. And that's been a really, really valuable lesson for me. Because I'm not afraid of those kinds of people. You know, when I see a guy who's using his position in a certain way, I know that if he walked into a strip club, it would take the girls all of half an hour to take him right down to fucking size. So those people don't scare me. Also, some men are so sweet as well, I'm not one to say like, *All men are bad.* I think I was quite frightened of men before actually, but now I can just see their insecurities.

· ·
·

How has it affected my relationships? I think a lot of dancers try to skirt this question. It's affected the kinds of men that I choose. I think when I first started dancing, I had a boyfriend who knew I was making a lot more money than him. I certainly didn't financially support him, but if there was a time when I'd have to pay an extra bit more than him, I would happily do it. So at some level, he was kind of going along with the fact that I had more money than him. And eventually what happened was, I honestly couldn't have an orgasm with that guy. I just couldn't find him attractive. Like, the role reversal killed the sex life for me. Then as a kickback against that, I ended up going out with a very, very wealthy guy. This guy had no problem with me being a dancer at all. But the thing is, what he would do is, if I was going to work he'd be like, Well don't go to work, just live off me. And he'd just transfer me money so I didn't go to work. So he was sort of buying me out of my job. And I wasn't hustling him for money not to go to work, I generally wanted to go to work, but he was stopping me just because he was a very needy, needy person. You know, if I was in any other normal job, he wouldn't be able to do that. And I think in the end, that created a power imbalance where he eventually nearly bought me out of my job completely. Again, the tables turned because I was living off him in the end. I wasn't working. And then I lost my identity and I ended up becoming sort of depressed. Because, you know, if you don't have to get up and pay bills … I'd just lost my reason to do anything. He didn't do it with bad intentions, he just wanted me with him *all* the time. I know I probably didn't give it the same credence as a career, you know. This is my job. This is what I do. But I didn't give it the same importance that I would have done if I had a 'normal' job.

And then the worst case was when I had a boyfriend who pretended he was fine with me being a stripper when he first got with me, but then as time went on and the relationship broke down, he sort of wore me down, and he started making a massive fuss about it. You know, complaining about me dancing, and he was saying, When are you going to get a proper job? And trying to look for careers for me, when actually he was shaming me. And because it was a very dysfunctional relationship, I really, really started taking some of that shame on. Then, consequently, when I was going to work, I wasn't really in it. And it cost me a lot of money and a lot of peace of mind. In the end, he turned out to be a horribly controlling boyfriend. He didn't want me to be independent. He wanted to take that away from me. I've also had the experience where I've been with a guy and he's been fine, but then when you finally have an argument, it gets thrown back in your face – Well you're a stripper! It gets thrown in your face like you're the worst of the worst. They'll use it as a stick to beat you with. I know now from experience, as soon as they say that, I'm gone. As soon as someone hits me with the stripper card, I'm like, Bye. See you. Because I never lied about it. Some girls lie to their boyfriends about what they do. I've never lied about it. And with those guys, it just means they never really respected you in the first place.

Bex

Bex

CLEO

I think being a stripper gives you empathy. People who act like arseholes – who I'd see in the street or at a bar and think, *Well you're obviously a twat* – sometimes they've just had certain events happen in their life and pressures from their family. They've ended up in these City jobs acting like arseholes and treating everyone around them like shit, but I don't see that they're innately bad people. This job gives you empathy for the arseholes of the world.

My first club was ████████████████. I was like 20 or 21. When I did my first stage show I was really nervous, but I also really enjoyed it. I wore this tacky stripper dress, this kind of long, gross leatherette thing. It's really weird because on stage you're wearing clothes that you wouldn't normally wear, and you have a different name – so it really is a performance and it doesn't feel like me. With the performing aspect of it I'm definitely being Cleo, because *I* would never go naked on a stage in front of people. If I'm being intimate with someone in bed, someone who I actually care for, I find being naked around them really nerve-wracking. Yet onstage I'm able to be naked in front of, like, hundreds of people sometimes. That part of it is quite enjoyable.

I think, initially, when I first started doing it, I really had to put myself into a different character because I kind of didn't believe that I was a stripper, it was just so surreal. Now sometimes, if I'm feeling quite vulnerable in my personal life, I like to play more of a character or role at work because it just gives me a break from being me, which sometimes we all need. I kind of tailor my personality according to the customer. After having worked in the industry for a number of years, I think that I've developed an ability to read into what people need me to be. For example, men who work high up in corporate industries or are generally the boss or own companies, they usually get off on being submissive, so I tend to be slightly more abusive towards them. It's kind of against my nature to be abusive or rude to people, or even come across as arrogant, but those are some of Cleo's characteristics.

Other times I feel like I'm not necessarily acting as a different person, but rather accessing a different part of myself. When it comes to the customers who continually come back, or with who I've had a really good rapport, it's because I'm being a certain version of myself that's really authentic. So we have a more genuine kind of connection because there's something honest there. Even though you're in a space where you're both suspending your disbelief, there still has to be something real about it.

It's very rare that I will do a dance for £20 ($27) where I work now. You're not supposed to charge more but why would I do that if I can get more. I'll normally just say to the customer, I'll be as generous with my body as you are with your pocket. I think it's just about making the rules work for you or, like, just being a little bit streetwise. Ultimately, we are self-employed and I certainly think that this kind of work should be on your own terms because of the nature of the job. So you kind of make your own rules, but just hide it well.

At ██████ where I'm working now, the private dancing is in a kind of long corridor with mirrors on the walls. It's got a kind of David Lynch vibe to it, it's quite sinister. Within an hour or two of the club being open – because the girls lean against the mirrors – there's like dirty handprints or arse prints smudged into the glass. From the customer's perspective it's like this really sexy, exotic space but the truth is, if you turn on the lights you'd probably want to get your hand sanitiser out.

Sometimes doing a private dance can be unnerving because, physically, you're quite vulnerable. You know, you've got your clothes off in front of a stranger in quite close proximity. And there have been instances where people have bitten me. I've turned around and then before you know it they'll have their teeth in my shoulder. That's happened to me a few times. I must look quite edible or something, people bite me a lot. So that kind of thing, obviously I don't enjoy.

. .
.

Why do I think men go to strip clubs? To feel like a man. To feel like a more appealing version of themselves. Because they don't want to always be the inadequate husband version of themselves.

I had a customer at ████████ recently who gave four of us each £2,500 ($3,500) just to do coke with him. It was actually quite scary because he was taking so much coke he started talking to this woman called Helen who wasn't there. Apparently he owns a big media company and he does this every few months. He's quite a well-known guy, late-thirties, early-forties, who does a lot of charity work and appears sane. But every few months he just goes completely mad, off on one. He looks just like a fucking respectable family man, so it's shocking that he behaves that way.

So this customer paid for all four of us all to leave the club and go into his office in Soho. Now, I'd never left a club before to go out with a customer. I know lots of people do, but I'd be scared that they'd expect me to have sex with them or that there wouldn't be the boundaries or protection of being within the vicinity of a club. But, because there were other girls present as well, I felt safe to do it. I didn't even know until then that the club had a secret backdoor, so the girls could just pay off the bouncer and leave out of the back. So we get to this corporate building, like this respectable-looking workspace, and there's fucking cocaine all over everyone's desks. And the way it works is, he wants to pay you but he'll be like, Okay I'll put another £1,000 ($1,400) in your account, but only if she stands in that corner and you have to hold her shoe on your head and then she has to turn her back. And then everyone will be like, Okay! And then he'll say, Actually, no, I want her in that room and you over there ... and it just goes back and forth like this for ages. It was like being in a video game, we were literally running from room to room for hours on end with this coked-up guy who kept turning the lights on and off. At one point he locked all of our handbags in one room and then gave us this massive box of keys and we were all in a line handing the keys over one by one and trying to get in the room, trying to find the fucking key to get our things back. Fortunately we did but it took like half an hour. It was a pretty crazy experience. Then we ordered takeaways, and he was just putting more and more money in our accounts while doing coke.

It's all about some weird power game where he likes having these girls around him and, you know, telling them to do fucking jumping jacks or whatever. So mental. By the end it got so late we were worried the cleaners were gonna come. And by that point he was in his office with the door shut and the lights off talking to this woman called Helen who wasn't there and we couldn't get him to leave. So God knows what they walked in on in the morning.

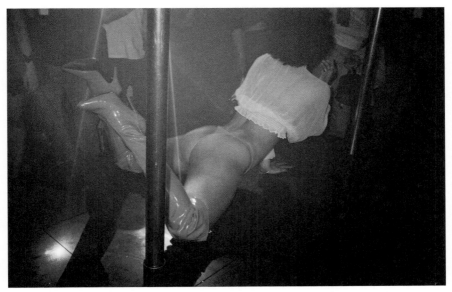

Venus

Venus

Venus

**HAVANA
GISELLE
AMY
LUCINDA
BEX
KATIE
PAIGE
AMÉLIE
SOPHIA**

THE

PRIVATE

DANCE

Bex

The dimly lit, closeted environment of the strip joint, with its darkened antechambers of booths, private dance areas, and VIP rooms, often feels like a confessional space where the exposure of our bodies somehow enables customers to reveal hidden aspects of their own selves.

Away from the main floor of the club, private dances sometimes become sit-downs if we strike it lucky. A well-established practice in bigger strip clubs, sit-downs have also begun to be a feature of many smaller strip pubs over recent years. Wherever possible, we sell our company by the hour (sharing a percentage of our earnings with the club) and, together, e while away intense periods in these windowless, intimate spaces. Sometimes, the entire time consists of inventively diverting customers from their own constantly thwarted desire. On other occasions, they know the score and everybody has fun. When the alcohol and the proximity of naked flesh seems to invite disclosure, customers often share their innermost secrets, whether we want them to or not – secrets that can be shocking, tedious, compelling, harrowing, hilarious, and everything in between.

Table dancing, as opposed to lap dancing, means no touching. In a private dance room, the customer sits in an armchair or a sofa while we perform a striptease on a nearby podium. Some clubs have a no-contact policy that can only be breached in subtle ways (a high heel may come to rest momentarily on the customer's thigh during a private dance, for instance). This is not to suggest we have any desire to transgress these rules – the code of conduct is part of the infrastructure that keeps us safe; we need to keep that boundary intact between ourselves and the customer. This boundary is not only our excuse for not touching them, it's also the customer's means of rationalising why we're not touching them; it enables them to maintain their suspension of disbelief. So, the challenge is to work within the rules to make the dance feel like a sexual encounter without any physical contact. It's about creating the illusion of proximity without touching – eye contact, provocative conversation, making them believe we're enjoying it as much as they are (sometimes we genuinely are. Sometimes we're thinking about what to cook for dinner).

WANTING YOU TO WANT ME

Customers are rarely drawn to strip clubs in search of actual sex. It's not always easy to explain why regulars spend their money on strippers when an escort may charge less by the hour for sex than we charge to provoke them and drink their Champagne. Maybe it's the suggestion of intimacy or sexual intrigue, safely circumscribed by the house rules. Maybe, because their desire isn't consummated, it's kept alive for longer: you can't desire something you already have, and you can never really *have* a stripper within the enchanted space of the strip club.

The mysterious dynamic between strippers and their loyal customers is hard to grasp, even from within. Most encounters are one-offs, yet some complex and surprising relationships can be spun out for months or even years with their mechanisms of fantasy, friendship, companionship, affirmation, addiction or lust intact.

Every dancer accumulates a wealth of odd, hilarious or macabre tales about clients, but for most, these sensational anecdotes are counterbalanced by genuine moments of rapport, friendship, and sympathy. For others, experiences in the world of strip clubs may have soured their relationship with sex and men altogether, and galvanising their existing beliefs that most people are cunts.

There's a huge amount of emotional labour involved in sex work. We are exhausted by smiling for hours, trying to please, laughing at jokes and anticipating desires. We may be fantasy technicians but we're also 'Care in the Community'.

Sometimes the customers are pure fantasists. Sometimes they're under no illusions whatsoever. The stereotype of the creepy customer does exist. But for every loner with unkempt fingernails whose interests are disconcertingly gynaecological, there are also customers with integrity, charm, and kindness. In reality, it's not easy to pigeonhole the people who frequent strip clubs or to guess their stories any more than it is to make assumptions about the dancers who work there.

Barbara

HAVANA

I had a very strange conversation with a guy the other day. He asked for his coat because he wanted to leave, and he basically said to me – something that we are all so familiar with hearing, all the time – Well, what's the point? No one's gonna love me here, are they? And I said, Well no, but if you came looking for that then of course you're going to leave upset. This is the problem with you men. This is what you forget. You come here thinking that you are going to be alright objectifying a woman, and then the strangest thing happens, which is that a lot of you suddenly realise you don't want to be objectified, either. So you leave very confused.

And the bottom line of all this mess is that no one wants to be objectified. No human being wants to be objectified. So the women come here thinking, *Alright, I'm conscious of this, so I'll be ok about being objectified because you're going to pay me money and that's the deal.* But it's the men that come in here and realise how much they don't want to be objectified. When they are thinking about themselves as just ... a consumer or a supplier of money, they start to think, *Hang on a minute, I actually would prefer to be appreciated for who I am. Why doesn't she like me?*

. .
.

First thing about Alan is, he gives me every kind of emotion possible, there's not one way to describe how I feel about Alan. He makes me feel this very difficult, knotted, convoluted labyrinth kind of thing of, *Oh my God this man needs saving.* I feel so sorry for him. All he needs is love. But at the same time ... he's just so easy to laugh at. That's the tragedy of him.

When I first started working at ███████, Alan only ever came to see this girl called Jenny. I actually think he believed that she was his girlfriend. In the early days he had that reputation of a guy that comes in the club – you know when a guy walks in and he's just got that thing about him where you knew that he was coming in as a big spender. You knew when Alan walked through the door, someone – and that someone was Jenny – was getting lucky that night, and every girl is like, *Ah I wish I was her!* He would come in and he would get all the drinks for everybody. Then he would go straight to VIP, sometimes VVIP, and stay there all night long. He would have the bucket with the champagne and everything. He was *that* customer.

I guess, because he was kind of in this very weird fantasy relationship with Jenny, she really had him round her finger. He would do anything for her. So no one else ever saw what Alan was really about. He was a bit of an enigma, basically. Alan was someone with money who was devoted to the girl who was extracting all that money out of him. Perfect customer. He was all of that.

When Jenny left the club three years ago, he sort of stopped coming but then gradually started to come back slowly and we were all kind of thinking, *Is he going to be that same guy?* Could we potentially be that one? Well, one night, I guess I thought I was getting lucky. Me and Anita took him upstairs.

I think that I would have been too scared to go near Alan on my own. But Anita and I made quite a good team. As much as she can be like a rival, an enemy, she's great to work with because she is really cutting about the time and the money. And I'm not good at being forceful like that – I'm all about the jokes and the distraction from the time and the money. So we're a good balance in a situation like that.

I think we were standing next to each other at the moment when we spotted him in the jungle and realised he was vulnerable. We looked at each other and were like, *Let's go*. We got upstairs. But the whole of those four hours just revolved around us two diverting him from everything that he was about, while at the same time trying to keep ourselves from laughing at the situation. I mean, he does all these weird, like, cat hisses and vampire growls. He wants to grab you. You don't know where his fingers have been. He's filthy, he's sweaty, he's smelly, he's on drugs, he's drinking, and you don't really want this man to be touching you. So everything is about treating him like a simple child and distracting him from all of these things. The dressing up box comes into play, we dressed him up in a wig and tutu. And he takes it, he just takes it. Because I guess he wants the attention.

My interpretation is that he's either got close to a woman once, or maybe a couple of times in his life if he's lucky, and he's never got over it because he can't repeat it. But if that's not the situation then I think he's never been near a woman so he's only ever fantasised about what he can do, or what he thinks is the ultimate experience for a woman to receive from a man. So that's the dominating topic of conversation, basically. Along the lines of – oh God, it's disgusting – it's about licking ... he just wants to tell you for hours and hours about his supposed expertise in licking pussy. And you know, it's not even just the talk about it. It's the constant ... it's the fucking licking of the thumb and middle finger together. Absolutely putrefying. So listening to that for four hours is really quite disturbing if you don't make light of the situation.

At one point I said, Oh, Alan! Shall we put some music on? Shall we play our own music? Because the DJ's playing some shit stuff tonight! Just to divert him. So he gets his phone out and starts asking us to listen to certain things on YouTube and it's all very ridiculous. Then we got into looking at his photographs and I just spotted this cat. And I said, Oh, Alan, is that your cat? Well, it opened a whole can of worms because one of his cats had died and he was devastated about that. And he starts getting very emotional ... oh dear, I can't even describe it. It's almost like he's so angry that you've even dared ask because it's going to open up a deep well for him.

We just kept flicking through the whole stream of photographs that he's got on his phone, and for me, I'm just watching the story of Alan's daily life unfold. What really goes on in this man's life. And I guess it just made me feel really sad. It was pictures of his cat, and it was pictures of him at a barbecue, which just looked like the most tragic affair ever – maybe him and one other person cooking a single sausage on a barbecue in the rain and in some absolutely derelict garden. And then we get these pictures of him wandering around a Sainsbury's supermarket – photographs of a Sainsbury's Basics microwave meal, Sainsbury's Basics lagers.

The best way to describe it is like playing psychological ping pong. That is it. The only way for you to sort of justify what you are being a part of is – I mean, for me, personally – keeping it as light and as funny as possible. But sometimes the dark part of it is, I realise I'm the only one laughing.

∴

There was another night that kind of blew my mind over what goes on in a man's psyche. It was this whole group, a handful of wealthy guys – bankers or whatever – and I was lucky enough to get in with one of them. I knew from the get-go that he was probably there for his mates and he wasn't necessarily there for himself, he was just going along with the jovial mans' night out kind of thing. He wasn't really into me; we were having a conversation and he was being polite just to go through the motions. But because of the consensus of the whole group, they went up to the VIP.

When we were in the VIP, obviously I was trying to dance for him and I was trying to hold his attention with all this seduction nonsense, but he just wasn't really having it. I guess that's the thing that we all go through isn't it? Trying to suss out exactly which card to play with them. You don't know if they want the sexy card, the seductive card, the friend card, the mother card, the dominatrix card, the submissive card or the flipping just-don't-talk-to-me card, the just-sit-there card. You just don't know. So, up in the VIP, I'm obviously playing out all of these things, trying, because he wasn't giving me anything. He would not engage with me, every question I asked was a one-word answer. And, in the end, I think it got so frustrating for me, and maybe it played on my own insecurity and paranoia a little bit, and I was just like, Don't you fancy me? Or something like that. And that's when the conversation started.

He said to me, No, no, no, you just don't understand. And I was like, Are you just kind of going through the motions? Are you just sitting with me 'cause you have to, 'cause your mates have come and you're with them? And he said, Well, no. It's really awkward ... the situation is, I'm this guy's client, potentially. I wouldn't choose to be here, but I have to because I'm his client and he's trying to entertain me. But, the thing I'm very conscious of, is that I don't want to be blackmailed and I don't want to be manipulated. And I was like, How is that possible if you're all doing the same thing? And nothing's gonna happen between us, we're just having a good time. And he said, I feel paranoid, basically, that if I'm seen by any of these guys touching you or engaging with you in any way, shape or form, then that's their weapon against me. In business between men, to manipulate you and get you to do something they want, they need to get you into a vulnerable situation where you lose your defences. Once you do something bad it's like a secret weapon against you. Then you leave the situation with an immense amount of guilt and, because you've shared that experience, and you've done something a bit untoward, you just feel compelled to then do business with them. Otherwise they've got that against you.

I was really taken aback because I had never seen it from their perspective before in that sense, and no other man had ever been able to explain that to me. If you think about the number of guys that we have encountered who just seem so offish and adamant that they don't want to be affected by a naked woman frolicking about, you realised that's their defence against that other man's weapon that they're trying to manipulate them with. It's all very underlying. But I guess, just on our part, it's something we might never easily understand.

• •
•

Funnily enough, all these little situations that I've ever been in – or the things that I remember – have all served to remind me of that mentality I've gone into the club with. I've gone in with the attitude of, *I don't want to really engage. I'm not here to make friends. I'm not here to understand you. I don't want you to understand me. This is about whether I can give you an objectified situation that you're going to pay me for. I want to get in and out, and I want to take the money.* And I guess that is probably, in conclusion, the whole conflict of the job for everybody who does it, at the end of the day. It's the fact that you go in there maybe with that feeling of, *Well, I know you're going*

to objectify me, but I'll go along with it because I need to earn a living.
So that is what I want to do. I don't want to give you anything extra.
I don't want you to give me anything extra.

It's awful that you go in there and take away your own – and
somebody else's – humanity. And the situations that you encounter
along the way are strangely never about anything sexual. You find
yourself in this moral crisis, because this person is kind of pulling on
your human strings and reminding you that, actually, yeah, this is what
life is really about. But it's not what I want to deal with in this context.

Barbara & friend

GISELLE

There are so many regular customers. Oh God, we could talk for days and days about them. So there was Martin, who I think had been in the army at some point and used to sort of salute people and pretend he was the most gentlemanly, chivalrous person in the world. He always dressed in a suit or blazer and pretended he had his own driver and was quite a big deal, but we all knew that the driver was just one of his regular cabbies. And when he wanted to dance with me or any of the girls, he'd go and wait for them at the stage at the end of their show and escort them, saying, Would you care to take my arm? Then he'd steer them to the private dance room, talking about how elegant they were or whatever. That's certainly what he did with me. He never paid particularly well but he did let me know how rich he was. I know that he helped some girls out a lot and, you know, helped to get their immigration statuses sorted out or something. He gave one of the girls away at her wedding. But also he was mental and enjoyed pretending to other customers that he owned the club. He really liked feeling important there, I guess because he didn't feel important enough outside. He was sort of a figure of fun in a way. But then when you really look back at a lot of these people you just think, *Oh gosh, that's kind of tragic.*

Then there was Angus. He always needed you to be in stockings because it reminded him of his first naughty sexual experience with an older woman who had shown him the ropes. He was fucked up. He was a real mess and a lot of work. And then there were the customers who were a lot of work because they were touchy-feely and it was horrible feeling their big hand on the small of your back. And I'd feel like, *They haven't done anything, they haven't groped me or anything, but it just feels invasive and it's not okay ...* it was weird trying to tread this fine line between wanting them to back off, and realising there wasn't anyone else in there you could make that much money out of. So you'd want to be able to keep the interaction going and resist alienating them by saying, Fuck off, you're repulsing me, you dick. But also, you don't want to feel repulsed. So how do you navigate this? And, more often than not, I just couldn't sustain it.

David was a properly fucking mad alcoholic. I first met him through one of the other girls he saw – Lola, with the huge tits that defied gravity. Unbelievable. Incidentally, she's living round the corner from my mum now and she's about to have another baby, so imagine how big her tits are now. But, yeah, she introduced me to David. He was her customer for a while.

He was a lawyer who did very, very well. At some point in his life he had been a huge success and it seemed like he was still somehow managing to function at work, but every time I saw him he was ... it's so difficult to describe him. Just nuts. He always dressed very well in a suit and, because he spent so much money there, he'd have his own table set out for him. The house mum would come and talk to him and hug him and spend time with him and he would call her 'Mum' and they'd chat amongst themselves about how much money was going to be spent that day. He always ordered white wine – he didn't like champagne – and they always had his bottles ready for him.

His marriage was breaking down. He always talked about his kids, about his wife. And he always insisted that the girls dance to very specific songs on stage. They were all songs that reminded him of his soon-to-be ex-wife, and they were always songs that were in no way suitable for sexy dancing. Like, one of his songs was 'Don't You (Forget About Me)' by Simple Minds and I can't hear that now without getting a sort of hysterical, traumatic recall.

Oh God, he would just talk endlessly without saying anything. He would make no sense. And then there were certain refrains he would just say over and over again. And so – this is why he really liked me and thought I was a cut above the rest – I clocked that he said the same thing every time and that he was usually so drunk that he wouldn't remember having said it before. So I went away, I Googled some of the stuff he said and when he came back next time I had references for it. He'd always say, Beauty is truth and truth is beauty. And I'd say, Isn't that Keats' 'Ode to a Grecian Urn'?

He was like, You are a cultured, cultured lady. I was like, Yeah it's just a thing I know.

One of his other recurring things was that he'd ask me, What are the major philosophies in the world? The first time he said this to me I'd be like, Okay, so, Stoicism, Hedonism ... and he was like, Nope! Religions. And so obviously next time he asks about the major philosophies I say, Judaism, Christianity ... and he says, You are switched on! Yeah, right, okay. And it would repeat and repeat. So it was a good year or so of having the same conversation. I was his perfect woman by the end of it. I mean, to the point where he asked me to move in with him!

He had been so eroded through years of abusing alcohol and his credit card. He was like a shell. He was like the Coliseum if it had been shat on a lot – something that used to be grand, but now was just, I dunno, covered in shit. It was really sad, but I met him in my last few years of working there and I just had so much else on my mind. I wanted to get out of there. So I was just so happy to get the money from him to begin with that I didn't really think too much about what was going on with him. And then, even being paid several hundred an hour just to sit and listen to the same thing, it became too much. It became such a chore.

It's funny actually, thinking about those sit-downs ... a 'sit-down' being when you're paid just to sit and chat with one of the customers and they agree to an hourly rate with you. And sometimes you'll do dances for them within that time and sometimes not, depending on what they want. The price is negotiated by you. Or, in the case of David, because he knew the house mum so well, it would quite often be negotiated with her. And there would be a sort of complicity there because she'd try to get as much money as possible. Sometimes, if she'd done a lot of the work as well, like if she'd sat with him for quite a while, I'd give her some of it as well.

The sit-downs are really where customers can start to see themselves as your partner. It starts out like they're your benefactor and then, depending on the guy – and the girl as well – they can carry on regularly for weeks. Or years! If someone comes in sporadically, then that can be sustained for years and it's not unhealthy – it's just

WANTING YOU TO WANT ME

sort of that the guy knows the deal and he doesn't *need* you, but it's just that he's well-off enough that he can afford to do that from time to time, and he enjoys it there. Like, it's just a bit of an escape or a luxury, like going and getting a massage or something. It's fun with those kinds of people but they are rare, they're really rare.

Always at some point it happens that the balance tips and they want something that you can't actually give them. They realise that this make-believe isn't actually gonna come true, and it becomes too sad or too pointless and hopeless. And so you're always wanting to be able to drag it out as much as you can, but then it gets harder and harder because you're having to listen to the same sort of shit over and over, and you've had so much time with this person that your mind starts to wander when you're with them. Because, you know, there is definitely an art to being able to spin the conversation that much, but you're just not using enough of yourself. Well, in my case, I just started finding myself thinking, *What the fuck am I doing?* I felt sad after too long doing sit-downs. I just felt like this isn't good for either of us. It didn't feel worth it anymore.

After I stopped working there I met up with David once and, oh, it was nerve-wracking 'cause he asked to meet at a restaurant that I knew the owner of the club went to quite often. And socialising with customers outside of work was forbidden. I was like, *Fuck, if she comes in* ... I didn't work there anymore but, still, I just didn't want that. So I sat there with him and it was really weird because I had just started seeing my boyfriend who happens to also be named David, and this David kept referring to himself in the third person, luckily. So he was asking me, Do you love David? And I said, Yes I do love David. I'm not lying in the slightest. I really, really do! So much! David's the love of my life! I could see myself having a family with David!

Anyway, then he put my finger in his mouth, which was really weird. He just held my hand and then – it was one of those things – I was sat there in a restaurant, i.e. in public, like, not in the club, and he just took my hand and put my finger in his mouth. And I was like, *Who am I? What the fuck am I doing here?* And it really, really freaked me out because here I was – me, not Giselle – realising, I'm sat in this restaurant with my finger in some weird old man's mouth.

Amélie

AMY

I picked 'Amy' because I just thought in every classroom across Britain there was probably a fit Amy, so I just thought men would connect with that. There must have been an Amy that they once fancied or a girl that they went out with, so I just went for something really normal.

Because I worked as a professional dancer before, I felt I'd been taught how to seduce people anyway, so it wasn't like this massive thing for me and I'm very comfortable being naked. But I did have a really weird notion as I was getting ready, studying my vagina, because I was like, *Is it weird?* I don't know, I hadn't shown it to that many men before so I spent ages studying it and questioning it. But, yeah, my first night was quite normal really.

I was 30 when I started but I looked a lot younger. And I think I was very sexually confident and a lot of the girls there didn't like it, they immediately were threatened. One girl tried to bully me a little bit and I basically told her about herself and then she had this epiphany. She was basically like, Look, you need to watch what you're doing, when you're doing sit-downs because you're messing it up. And I was like, What's your problem with me? And she was really taken aback because I think she thought that I was going to be scared. And, yeah, so I had to control that situation a little bit – playground tactics. But now I'm really good friends with that girl so it's fine.

One of my first nights I made, like ... I made a lot of money. I did six hours in VIP straight. But it's definitely a new girl thing – it's like being fresh and it's exciting but, like any job, the novelty wears off after a bit, so your earning potential goes down. But for me personally it's always better than any other normal job that I've had under a capitalist structure where I've worked for a big corporation. Getting paid £10 ($14) an hour and being treated like shit has been way more humiliating than anything that I've done in dancing.

I wear a wig because I transform into a different version of myself. I perform my sexuality very, very differently in the club to how I do outside in the street. I do that as a weapon. You know, it's a tool to extract money out of men.

I remember having a really weird night with a very, very young boy who was like 21. You don't normally get boys of that age in there. We went upstairs, and there's a fancy dress box there, so he picked out this really ugly dress that was pink and floor-length and was like, I want you to put this on and we're just gonna look at girly stuff on our phones and we're gonna pretend that we're going shopping. And I was like, Right, okay. And he was a sissy, and he kept using lines from *Mean Girls*. He was like, Oh my God, don't you think this is so fetch! Isn't this so cute! Oh my God, girly stuff! Girly stuff! And we did it for three hours. It was a really, really weird experience. And then he kept going on about how he wanted to shit in his nappy and he wished that I could change his nappy and all this stuff. And it was the most not-sexual experience ever. I didn't take my clothes off, I just sat in this pink taffeta ball gown. So that was weird because I'd never really met someone that young who expressed their sexuality like that.

I've had one guy that all he wanted to do was talk about getting fucked in the arse by big Black dick. He kept saying, I just wanna get fucked in my arse, do you think that's weird? And I'm like, Babe, I don't think that's weird, whatever floats your boat. But I feel like with that community of men there's a really insidious, almost like colonial desire – like they haven't decolonised their desire, they've got these very strange notions of what they think is 'other' and 'taboo'.

That was a big thing that I realised, is a lot of these men have a lot of money and a lot of power, but they're very, very lonely and sad. I don't feel sorry for them in any way, but it was an eye-opener. I mean, obviously there needs to be a sexual emancipation of these men because, in turn, it will be better for queer people, it'll be better for sex workers, it'll be better for women in general. These men are not expressing their sexuality like they need to. So, in turn, that always turns into violence against the other sex. Which is why, I think, particularly the realm of stripping and sexual fantasy – adult sexual fantasy – is very important. People need to sort that side of themselves out for society to be better, you know?

There's a lot of men that I know are gay but, because of their situation, there is just no way they're allowed to express that. And I think, yes, sometimes you do get customers that are there trying to prove to themselves that they're not gay, massively. And that's why they cane it, kind of lose who they are, and then we're there to listen to it. And we're the only person that they can trust to talk to about it, and they go, Am I weird? And you go, No, you're not weird. And that's what they're paying for. They're not paying for my sexuality, they're paying for someone to go, No, you're not weird, it's alright.

One man told me this story about when he was a kid, that him and his neighbour went upstairs into their attic and they, like, they were 10 years old or whatever, and they touched each other with ribbons for hours. And I was like, *Oh God, that's so, so cute, actually.* But it is sad. But it's hard to feel bad for white straight men with loads of money and power.

I had this one guy who used to come and see me, who cross-dresses behind his wife's back. His fashion icon is Kat Slater from *EastEnders*, and he actually calls himself Anna Slater. I hadn't seen him for ages and then he came in and he looked quite thin and a bit weird, and I was like, Are you alright? What's happened? And he's like, My wife found my clothes that I dress up in. She threw me out. And I haven't really got any money so I decided to become a sex worker as Anna. And I was like, Woah! So how did you find that? He was like, You know, sometimes I enjoyed it, sometimes I didn't. I put an ad in a paper and booked a hotel room and just had sex with myriad men. And I was like, *Whoa, that's a big jump. You've gone from privilege to completely marginalised in a week.* And he looked a bit shook up by the whole thing to be honest, but I did enjoy talking to him about his experience as a cross-dresser because he'd be like, You know, I go and see these men who are straight, and I like it when they stand me up because it makes me feel more like a woman. And I was like, That is so loaded. So your idea of a woman is someone that gets treated badly. So when you dress as a woman, if you get treated badly by a straight man, you feel more woman. How fucking complex is that? But he definitely gets turned on by women as well. He likes to have dances and stuff, but he always says, I wish I was you, I wish I could do what you do. So that's really complex what's going on there.

I think it's really interesting though, because to me, it blows up the idea of gender and the performance of gender. Everyone actually wants to access both areas – male and female – whenever they want, and we can, if it's accepted. But it's only really in the realm of adult fantasy sex where people can really play with that. Although we are now seeing more discourse around it, with this younger generation of youth being like, you know you can access sexuality in so many different ways. Or you can access gender in so many different ways.

Recently what's been happening is I've been having a few female clients. There was one girl that came who was obviously having sex with her boss. The boss paid for me to go up with both of them, and then I got on with her so well and she was really hot. And he left because he got pissed off, and she carried on paying. And I was like, *This is what I wanna see in this realm: women with high-powered jobs coming to spend time with me and drinking champagne and whatever.* That's when I start being a bit buzzy about the whole situation. I'm like, *This is really fucking cool, actually.* And that's happened three times now, with really attractive women as well. I think because now I am bored with the male aspect of it, I do make a beeline if there's a woman in there just because I know it's gonna be a bit of a different experience.

. .
.

I definitely have a type of customer. It has to be someone that can talk about art, music, or some kind of philosophy. I have one guy that literally emails me about art and we talk about art. He's taking me to see that Rothko play in a month and he'll pay for me. But then sometimes it does get a bit weird ... I think maybe when you show your intelligence you're showing quite a big part of yourself. So then when it comes to the stripping bit sometimes it can be a bit clunky for me. So I have to be careful. Because we've just had this really intense conversation for an hour but at some point I need to take my clothes off. Amy shouldn't always show that side but sometimes she does because ... I just wanna talk to someone.

I like to be one-on-one and I like to connect with someone in some way. And that's it. I definitely don't ever go near anyone from Essex, I hate Essex boys. I can't connect with them, they've got no sense of humour. If you pick at their ego it crumbles in a second and they get quite aggressive. I can't be near anything like that because I will tell them to fuck off.

Working at ████████ was the first time I think that I'd really seen a real representation of female bodies. Because there was all sorts of shapes and sizes there and it wasn't really about, like, Western beauty ideals because the 'fittest girl' wouldn't necessarily earn the most money. It was all about performance. That's what I realised about sexual attraction – it's a performance. And it's got nothing to do with what the media is telling you – the rules kind of go out the window there.

I'm a woman of colour, but I pass with my wig on. With those bankers there is a lot of racism, and they don't necessarily deal with it very well. I pass as white. So, like, you know, I'm in there at a point of privilege.

I do think a sex club can be a real intense reflection of what's going on in society among certain groups. Because this is very much one class of man, so it's like this paradigm of what's going on at the top of British society. Isn't it Freud, or whatever other psychoanalysts, who say that whatever is going on in the bedroom or in sexual fantasy shows how healthy we are as a society? And I'm not sure British society is that healthy considering.

Before I started dancing I was having a problem of like, getting in arguments in the street with men that were looking at me, and I was getting in people's faces. My partner was worried saying, You need to stop doing this because something's going to happen. And then, when I started to dance, I realised it's not that they're exerting power, it's that they're actually so repressed in their expression of their sexuality that they have to look at me to cement their existence. And that's really, really pathetic, and weak; that you can't go past me without acknowledging that you think you're gonna fuck me or whatever – you know you're not, so it's really sad because you might die tomorrow and that's how you're living your existence. You're not emancipated. So once I realised how much power female sexuality holds, now I just don't get angry. I'm like, *Ahhh … you're living a really, really limited existence*.

From my experience as a sex worker I think, they're just not living … it's not power, it's weakness – they're weak. And it's really sad, but kind of hilarious as well. You see it everywhere, in anything that's a toxic masculine realm. Like in football, you see this really homoerotic violence that goes on is more about wanting to touch each other, really; it's more about wanting to get close to each other. And the fashion that goes along with it – the diamonds and this really homo-erotic, preened, femme-facing fashion … it's all about suppressed homosexuality and toxic masculinity.

Amy

Amy

LUCINDA

I was living in the States working as a journalist, and I really wanted to go on staff. I'd been freelance for a long time and I was just busting to be part of a team and have a regular wage. So I was like, *Alright, If I don't find a job by June 2006 I have to go back to England.* So, anyway, June came and went and I was like, *Fuck, no work.* So I looked on another part of *Craigslist* and I saw this job – 'Be a ballroom dance instructor. No experience required.' I thought, *Oh alright, I'll give it a go.* So I ended up taking the ballroom dance thing, which was such an assault on my self-confidence because I'm not a trained dancer! Anyway, it was an amazing experience in retrospect. They're part of a well-known worldwide franchise and their system is about bringing dance to the masses so that everyone can dance. And as an instructor you actually also train on premium customer service, which is where I got a lot of my ideas for stripping from.

So then what happens in some of my VIPs is I'm like, *Right, okay I need to soak up time, so fuck it, let's just dance.* And the customer would be like, I can't dance! And I'd be like, Give me five minutes and I'll show you the basics. And they loved it. 'Cause I do passionately believe that everyone should feel empowered by dance. And a lot of guys feel they can't, but they can.

So fast forward a few years and I'm seeing this guy who, classic story, he started to go nuts about me stripping and it just got really fucking intense and it really made my life hell. It was torture. He said I needed to stop dancing, and I was so broken at this point I agreed. I kept looking for other things but, you know, I can't take a job that's £10 ($14) an hour – I'd need to work 70 hours a week 'cause I live in London. So, what the fuck what am I going to do? Then I hatched this idea to try to convert my regular stripping customers into dance students. I charged them like a peep show model, so it was a pound a minute. What I did was I repurposed what I'd learned at the ballroom dance place. My pitch was this: Want to be able to dance with any woman, anywhere, to any music? So I got some of my regulars, the veteran pub goers and, you know what? They loved it. It meant we got to hang out and be silly *and* they all know how to dance now. I was doing that for about a year and a bit and, as part of the program, I would take them out dancing in central London, it was like their training wheels. And, you know, they were all so dedicated. I'm really proud of them.

I basically took the methodology from this company, but I've kind of fine-tuned it so people will get up and running really quick, just for really basic social dancing. They're not going to look technically professional, but they can have fun and they can do the leading, which is what intimidates them. And, you know, I really do love my guys and I appreciate them stepping out and having a go. I sometimes brought in guest teachers and I properly tried to make it a well-rounded program. And I occasionally flashed my bra at them, just to keep them interested.

Trixie

BEX

Well, with the private dances, it used to be a lot easier to keep people on repeat dances because you could make a bit of contact. And you know, if you could sit on someone's lap, you've basically got them until they lose the boner, which could be four or five dances later. These days, without that, it is more difficult. They have to slightly fall – not fall in *love* with you, but just slightly *fall* for you. You can't just do it on the basis of them getting their cock a bit hard.

In terms of the dance, it's called a striptease because you're just teasing. If you do everything straight away, you're giving all your cards up. You have to start slowly and work your way to eventually right at the end of the dance when you're probably doing the most explicit thing, and that is when you ask them for a repeat dance. You don't, you know, bend over and spread your legs within the first 10 seconds. Because then by the end they've already seen it and got accustomed to it. I see girls doing far too much on stage. You know, if you're showing people everything on stage for free, all you're doing is cheapening it for yourself and all the other girls. Like, it's about leading people on.

I've been doing it so many years and I'm reading people a lot, so I can see, or just kind of intuitively feel, when they're getting more turned on. They might be an arse guy, or a tit guy, or they're in love with you, or they're really dominant and want you to be on your hands and knees, or they're a submissive type and they want you to stand over them and tell them off ... you have to get really good at reading people 'cause the dances are always different. I think that's kind of the beauty of being a really good stripper, it's being able to, without a lot of explanation, read people and accurately predict what their sexual fantasies might be and then portray that to them. It's like a sex witchcraft.

What's my favourite customer? I guess the ideal thing that happens is you meet a customer who matches the mood that you're

Bex

in. So, if I'm feeling premenstrual and I'm really kind of angry and snapping at people, if I meet a guy who wants to be spoken to like shit, you know, it's a win-win situation for the both of us. And I definitely like the older men who like the idea that they're spoiling you. Because they know that you're playing them and they like being played. That's the dynamic I like the best. They understand the business and they appreciate the work that you're doing and they're happy. They enjoy indulging you, and that, for me, is the best customer. I also prefer quality rather than quantity. I prefer a few customers who are all engaged rather than a busy Friday night where the place is packed but everyone is pissed and it's hard to get anyone's attention. And on a busy Friday or Saturday night it's generally big groups of lads, and even if they did really like your stage show, they don't necessarily want to go for a dance because they're frightened of doing anything in front of their mates. Don't underestimate how embarrassed guys get in strip clubs in front of their mates. It's a strange group dynamic. I think there's a perception of strip clubs, like it's always guys just going, whoa! But a lot of them come in with a lot of fear. I prefer a quiet Monday full of old men over a busy Saturday night any day.

The day shift customers are different. You get the men who are regulars and they've been coming for years. This truly is their social life. I mean, when you're in a strip club at three o'clock on a Tuesday afternoon, there's a small number of girls and it's the same girls on every shift, so they get to know all the girls. They start to feel like the club is like their family and they love that because they get a sense of belonging somewhere. Some of them are probably misfits in other areas, but they gain acceptance in a place like ▆▆▆ because it's full of complete outliers. Also, the ones who come in on the day shift, they've purposefully come to us. You don't end up in a strip club at that time of day by accident, like, you know what you're doing. So I generally find it easier to work with them, they know the deal. A lot of the time on the night shift you get guys who have been dragged along on a lads' night out and they've got a girlfriend and they don't really want to be there, or they don't like strippers, or they're just a total misogynist and they hate the idea that they're going to get taken for a ride by a girl. So yeah, there is definitely a difference. It's more targeted on the day shift. There's less girls and less competition. I'm not gonna say we're lazy but, it's ironic – on a day shift, the less we pressure people, the more they spend. They come in because they want to come to the strip club, not because they couldn't get into Bar Rumba, you know? And they appreciate what we're doing.

∙ ∙
∙

The private dancers are so sedate over here, they're not really full-on. In New York, you'd be straight-up grinding on people's laps, and if you're with an attractive person you'd be turned on because you know, you've been crawling all over their lap for ages, which is great 'cause you just end up charging them more and more and more money. But the way that we're dancing here, the dances are so fucking far away, they're air dances – there's no contact whatsoever and there has to be a visible space between the customer and performer. So you'd really have to have chemistry with someone to be turned on.

It only happened once in 14 years. A guy with boobs, but it wasn't a guy … it was an intersex person. I was at ███████ in Soho, which is a terrible club, and this person walked in and it was like the elephant in the room. I thought, *I'm either going to address the fact that you're a guy with tits, or we're just not going to mention it*. Do you know what I mean? 'Cause these weren't small tits, this was a big pair of knockers, right? And then eventually I just said, Listen, I'm just gonna come out with it, okay. What's going on? And then they said, Yeah, I'm both. And we got into a big discussion about it. I said, Do you intend to have surgery? And they said, No. I accept myself how I am and that's how I was made. And for me, that kind of confidence was very, very sexy. Very, very sexy because to be so far out from the norm and to have embraced it, is like … how do you get more confident than that?! And then I eventually took them for a dance and I was like a kid in a candy shop. I'm seeing male and female at the same time in one person and, being bisexual, that just completely tipped me over the edge. I couldn't … I was like, *Tits!* And then I turn around and there's a dick going on too, and with the male *and* female

Bex

energy ... my head was spinning. I tell you what, I would've fucked them and sucked them and got their tits in my face. I'd have been there all day and all night long in a total frenzy. It was like everything at once. I was like, *This is great!* A very underrepresented section of society, but don't knock it until you try it. The intersex dance, the best dance ever. I was absolutely turned on, I realised something about myself sexually that I didn't know. I could have had an orgasm in 30 seconds flat.

: :

Some of the clubs I've been in can be deeply toxic work environments. If you're already susceptible to problems with drug use or drinking, or even just sort of impulsive, wild behaviour, it's like putting lighter fluid on it.

Before, the dances were closer and it was more about the dancing. Now it's got stricter with the dancing, and girls are having to find other ways to make money. And, for me, I made a lot of money just partying with people and sniffing coke. You're not really a stripper anymore, you're basically a glorified drug dealer. You're encouraging guys to take drugs and then taking it with them for hours on end. There's something really, really draining for the soul about that kind of drug use. And it's just not why I got into the game. I got into it because of all the performing, you know. I liked the fun, not because I wanted to be in that kind of state, risking my emotional and physical health to make money. Also, those kinds of clubs that encourage that kind of behaviour, they tend to be the ones that are taking a lot of commission and where the whole environment becomes massively toxic.

There's no way of knowing whether I'd have had a drug problem if I hadn't worked in strip clubs, but I've got to say, for me, it just enabled me at that point. I got trapped in this absolute loop of just getting off my nut at work. It took away a few years of my life, and that was horrible. No amount of money is worth doing that. I thought the money was making it worth it, but in the end I was so shattered that I lost all the money just getting well.

There are people who come with really difficult circumstances to this job – we can't pretend it's all like freedom fighters and that we're all here coming up roses. Like there is some dark stuff going on, and that's just in London, I mean, God knows what's going on in the rest of the UK. And it's the way that certain clubs are run. It's the VIPs and the commission structures that I think have a big effect on it. When stripping first started in this country it was never about VIPs, that's something that came later. Strip clubs worked very, very well without VIPs – their introduction, on the whole, created a lot of division between the girls and led to these kinds of problems.

∴

One thing that really interested me was when we thought we might not get the license renewed at ██████ and how emotionally invested we all were in it. You know, just how upset everyone was at the thought of it not being there anymore. The council are coming down on the strip clubs but because ██████ has been there so many years, it usually goes through fairly easily, but this year we had more trouble with it. A lot of council visits, tightening up on the rules, and the word on the grapevine was that we were not going to get the license renewed. And there's been a lot of women's groups protesting against strip clubs and it's a very contentious issue at the moment. We were kinda preparing ourselves for the worst and feeling really upset, like there's an emotional attachment to that place. I think if they had closed, there would've been a really terrible grieving process to go through. It wasn't just the thought of losing your job, but losing this slice of history in the middle of Soho that's just so unlike anywhere else. It seemed so unfair and so short-sighted to remove it.

We were worried we'd lose the license over the dancing. The girls were watching each other like hawks to make sure nobody did a 'naughty' dance. At some point, it got quite heated with people being accused of doing this or that. The couple of girls that *did* do stuff that wasn't allowed ended up getting fired. It's definitely tightened up a lot in there because of that. It seems to me at the moment we've got this massive, you know, fucking hashtag MeToo, and women's

WANTING YOU TO WANT ME

rights and everything, but in reality, it's like women's rights for good women, but the sluts ... I don't know, there seems to be this massive division at the moment between these feminist factions. All I want to do is get my tits out and make money, you know?

Anyway, we did get the license renewed and there was such a massive sense of relief.

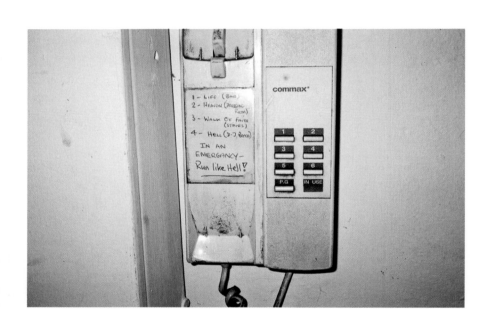

Bex

Bex

Bex

Bex

Bex

KATIE

Okay, so the story about the knickers ... I hadn't been dancing very long and I was working at ▮▮▮▮▮▮ and I was doing a private dance for this sort of caricature, grotesque strip club customer. It was like he'd been cast as the most archetypical, creepy, obese punter. He was middle-aged, but you kind of got the sense that perhaps he still lived at home. A slightly tragic figure, but also horrible. Quite dislikeable.

I was doing this private dance for him and I'd bent over on the podium and pulled my knickers down, and then I'd kind of flicked them with my heel and they'd landed next to him on the sofa. At some point in the dance I had my back to him and when I turned round my knickers were in his mouth. He'd stuffed the whole pair of knickers into his mouth. There was just a bit of the waistband kind of poking out, but his mouth was absolutely full of knickers, stuffed in like a gag. And he was sat there quite calmly, to all intents and purposes quite normally, as if nothing had happened.

I was horrified. They were these really beautiful Agent Provocateur knickers. You know, like years ago when Agent Provocateur was really good? Pink and black chevron silk, one of the first really expensive sets of lingerie I'd bought as a dancer. Anyway, like a schoolteacher I shouted, Get those out of your mouth! Like you would speak to a dog. And he didn't take them out with his hand, he just pushed him out with his tongue, so they flopped down onto his lap. I was absolutely revolted.

Obviously, I brought the dance to an end and I took the money off him. He was slightly disgruntled that he hadn't got the full duration. But then, what was *really* horrible – and I can still recall the feeling of it – is that, in order to get to the changing rooms from the private dance area, you had to walk through the whole club, and it's quite a big club, so I had to put the knickers back on. As I was walking I could feel the soggy fabric against me, the wetness of them. It felt absolutely revolting. I could feel his saliva on them as I was wearing them. The moistness of him. It felt like a horrible violation.

To get to the changing rooms there's these really treacherous steps that I'm absolutely amazed no girls killed themselves on while I was working there, especially tottering down there with their six-inch stripper heels on. They were really dangerous. But I just remember the fire door closing behind me, and I just stood at the top of the stairs trying to get the knickers off as quickly as I could. Suddenly they'd gone from these really precious, revered new pair of knickers that I loved, to holding them like it was an offensive object. It was really sad. It really ruined those knickers for me.

You do become quite desensitised to weird shit and to other people's quirks and fetishes. And to them imposing their sexuality on you. Them being turned on, in of itself, sometimes can be disgusting when you're not. When you're performing for someone and they're being aroused by it, you know that they're projecting something on you, they're thinking about you in whatever way, and you're perhaps not even thinking about them at all. You have to have your psychic protection in place to not feel the imprint of their gross thoughts that they're thinking as you're dancing for them. But to actually feel his saliva on my knickers ... it was almost worse than if he'd touched me with his hand or something. Once or twice I've been touched inappropriately while I've been dancing and it wasn't as bad as the thing with the knickers. For sure.

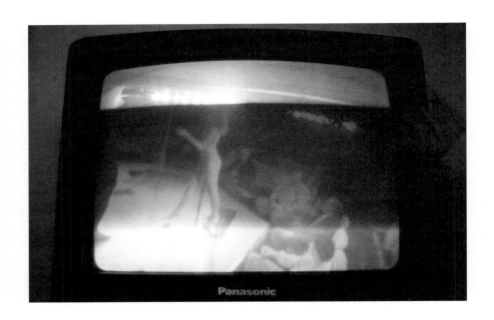

PAIGE

So I got fired. But then I had to come back in for 'a talk'. I had to watch five minutes of myself on CCTV. I remember seeing my customer come up, doing a line on camera. Like, *Phew – it wasn't me*. And then I got this look, like, Just wait. And there I was. Everything in front of the camera. My first thought was, *I look hot! That looks so hot*. I was just caning it and dancing. Head on – tits, bum, everything in front of the camera. So, I was sat there with the manager and with ███ and, bless her, she actually took half the blame because she was there, too, and she didn't tell me to stop. He said how disappointed he was, how he sees us as family, and I could have nearly got the club shut down. It was my regulars who were used to doing it up there because it used to be the blind spot. I just happened to get in there just after they had the new camera fitted and not told me.

They told me I was on a coke ban forever. So I made little coke pockets in all my bras because I knew they'd be checking my bag and my knickers and stuff like that. I was a raging cokehead back then. But I swear when you go upstairs, the walls stink of coke. I'm like*, It's in there somewhere, how do we get to it!?* I can hear it and I can smell it.

I didn't go in at the start with the aim to do it, but then you make new friends and they're all pretty and they're offering you coke in the toilets and you're like, *Oh, it's so tempting!* So, yeah. And then you meet customers who do coke and the only way you can listen to their bullshit is by getting high with them. Because coke chat is the most boring thing. Ever.

One night I made £5,000 ($7,000). It was my best night. But I spent the whole night talking to this guy who was just like, Tell me you love me! Please, tell me you love me, don't you love me? And that was probably the most exhausting night, even though he wasn't pervy or too grabby. It was just the need for intimacy. Very, very needy. And that was tough. Everyone I had was a little bit quirky. We had one guy who listened to *Swan Lake* and wanted us to dance in feathers and he'd be the black swan. He would dress up as a chicken and have two of us dancing. That was quite fun. Another guy in one of the clubs fantasised about being in a bath full of custard. And those onesies. I've made so much money just dancing in a dinosaur onesie for seven hours. Or just playing sword fighting with whips and stuff. It's ridiculous. I had one regular who claimed to be a porn director. Came in with a Hawaiian T-shirt on and checkered trousers and told me he was a porn director. But then it turns out he told me a different lie every time he came in. Actually, he works in printing and he was just a raging cokehead. So every time I was with him, all we'd do is loads of coke. And he had quite good coke.

Most of my regulars were there for me, but I used to try to get other girls in just so I didn't have to deal with them on my own. Apart from when Sam was my regular, obviously, and I started falling in love with him. If the other girls had gone near him I would have been fuming.

Sam was the quickest VIP I ever had. I literally just walked up to him, and he's like, Let's go upstairs. We talked and I had butterflies in my stomach like I've never had at work. It was a really weird thing. Then I found out that he had a kid, and he was still living with the mum but, you know, going through tough times, not together … I wrote him off at first. Then he kept coming in for about … four months? And then eventually, I think we were just like Fuck it, let's meet before work, and we went for a drink. I remember seeing him in his suit and just being like, *Wow. He's just, like … my heart is going!* We would talk about everything. He'd never push me to take my clothes off, or do this or that. We just used to talk. Really, really deep. We did do a lot of coke together.

One thing led to another. I was drunk, and I thought we were going back to a hotel, but he took me back to my house and I was really embarrassed because I was living in this little attic in Islington. Then we saw each other every Tuesday after that. Every Tuesday night we'd meet up, we'd go for drinks, we'd chat, we'd get high and then we'd have crazy sex back in my little flat. After a while we started to have feelings for each other. And then it got tough. It got tougher and tougher and tougher. And then I found out on Facebook that he'd got married to the mother of his kid and I basically had a breakdown.

We'd been seeing each other for a year. We'd already fallen in love and been on holiday together by then. I wasn't going to let him back in my life. But he was very, very pushy and he convinced me that he was going to leave her. But he was taking too long and I told his wife because I just couldn't take it anymore. I actually told her to get out of the relationship because I thought if I told her about us then he'd tell me to fuck off. But that wasn't the case. Still. We still loved each other. It was like literally nothing was able to tear that apart because we had such strong feelings.

Dancing just became impossible. Like, when you're in love with someone, especially because I met him there – it just became impossible. When he did leave her, he just hated me being at the club, he'd want me home straight away. He'd be texting me constantly while I was there. So I ended up just stopping dancing for him and, yeah, I was happy. But the drugs didn't stop. And that was the main reason – one of the reasons – I wanted to stop dancing, was because of the drugs.

So then I lived with him and I was broke and I was unhappy, and I couldn't concentrate on what I wanted to do. I thought, *I'll give up dancing for him*. But then, they don't realise that when you're stopping dancing it's not as easy to go into another job as you think. Because you're dealing with confidence issues, you're dealing with, *What the fuck do I put on my CV?* It takes time. And I feel like there's been a lot of pressure on me to keep another job. But at the same time, I'm in this destructive relationship where there's drugs and alcohol, and I've lost jobs because of that. I am not blaming him for that but, you know, it was like ... I wanted to stop. I wanted to stop everything toxic. I just wanted to teach yoga and I wanted to concentrate on acting, which were two things I loved. I decided that those were the two things I was going to concentrate on, like, years and years ago. And that's all I've wanted to do. But I have found that everything's been a hindrance. It's not even the dancing, it's the drugs and alcohol that comes with it that's the problem. I'd happily go back and dance if I knew I wasn't going to be taking drugs. Dancing on a pole is fun. It's glamorous. And it's nice getting all dressed up. It's really nice. And I've made very good friends there. And people are a bit more real. It can be a laugh.

Well, obviously what I thought would happen, happened. And I left the love affair with nothing. So yeah, probably I'm going to go back to stripping. But I'm going to go back into it with a different attitude, an attitude to stay healthy.

It's been a long fucking road and I just felt like, as much as I've tried to heal ... something like that ... it just hasn't healed. I've probably not loved anyone as much as I loved him, which is why it's been so painful. Serves you right for having an affair, innit? An affair. That you didn't know was, you know, an affair. So it's taken its toll and it's been tough. A lot of the time, I've felt like the bad person. I'm the stripper who tore him away from his life, even though I didn't know the extent of it. And, you know, a lot of the time the people around him are quite ... you just know you're being judged. Our relationship got quite ... it had a lot of pressure on it and it's gotten quite nasty. Because of that, there's been a lot of shouting, a lot screaming, a lot of drugs, a lot of things being twisted.

And it's tough because you do feel like his wife gets so much respect and a part of you is always going to feel like, *I'm the girl that can be chucked out ... because he met me in a strip club.* Even though you know you've got just as much to offer as these other women. And half the strippers you work with are way more intelligent. They work for themselves, they're creative. There's a lot of nice girls there and there's a lot of really talented girls. Girls who start businesses. Girls who've written their own play. And you're being judged by wives who are sat at home living off the money of the same guys who are paying us our money, but we're actually working for it.

． ．
　．

Doing a normal job ... and the concept of having a boss ... I went to work at this new members' club and the way they shout at you! I think it was the interior designer there, he just shoved me out of the way as if I was so below him. It was unbelievable. So I realised that sometimes you get more respect being in a strip club because somebody's going to stick up for us. Whereas in those normal jobs – one of the barmen pinned me up against the wall and then someone says, Oh you've got to get along with him, he's your boss. I'm just like, *Er, no I fucking don't*. When men do that to me I push them off. That's what I do. And I'm always going to do that, whatever environment I'm in. And in environments where you are actually *told* you can't stick up for yourself – it's actually worse.

Oh, I've punched guys. I got fired from ████████████ for punching a guy repeatedly in the face for trying to shove his fingers in my pussy. He did it forcefully and it really pissed me off. I punched him once and it wasn't enough so I punched him again and again until the bouncer told me to stop. I think I had just had it. And all my money had been stolen just before that as well, by a customer who had a dance with me and stole all the cash out of my bag. So I had just fucking had it.

There's nights you have guys that are just constantly grabbing you. I mean, men try to touch a woman who's naked, it's just their nature. But once you've told them no, they need to respect that. There was this one guy who kept grabbing my nipples, and you know when you're on your period and your nipples hurt? He was like, Darling, if you don't want me to touch your nipples then you're in the wrong job, aren't you? And I was like, Fuck off, cunt. I'm not being paid for you to touch my nipples. I had another guy who told me to say that I was 15 and he was my headteacher. So yeah, I definitely had the paedo experience. What I did is, I knew he was spending a lot of money and I got my friend to come up with me who is quite feisty. Basically, I just abused him and took his money. Because he's a paedo. If you can abuse anyone, you can abuse a paedo. I didn't like that night, that really freaked me out actually. It freaks me out to know people like that exist. It makes me so fucking angry. So. Fucking. Angry.

We hear things that no other women would hear from a man. They seem to think that there's some kind of cut-off point of how to speak to women, but you can just say anything to a stripper. They'll tell you anything, they'll tell you the tricks they use so that their wife doesn't find out, like pouring a fucking packet of cheese and onion crisps over their heads so they don't stink like fucking perfume when they go home. And this obviously affects you in relationships. They'll just tell you how they lie and you think, *Fuck, is that happening to me?* Because, obviously, their wife doesn't see that version of them. And you're wondering, *What version do I not see of whoever I'm with?*

So it obviously gives you a distorted image of men. You see men at their worst. You can see their best, too. You can have a great time with them. Some of my customers have really good banter. Some of them just dance like an idiot and you have a better party than you'd have with a boyfriend because nobody cares what they look like, or feel like, and you're stripping and you're naked and you don't give a shit. I've had nights where I've just been jumping on the sofas to Disney songs with my friend. I remember being like, He's gone to the toilet, quick, put *Frozen* on! Little did you know, he's going to come in and join us and we're dancing to *The Lion King* all night.

I found playing hard to get was the way forward. Just kind of letting them come. As soon as I started getting desperate for money and chasing them, it was like, No. Because you don't chase the man; men are hunters at the end of the day. So it works the same in stripping, I think. Unless you're the feisty kind of stripper who can be the mean girl, but I wasn't that. So I used to just kind of sit there and they would want me. And then, after a while, as I became more dead about dancing, they saw me as boring and they didn't really want me. So I think it's all to do with what you put out there – whether you are happy doing it, what energy you give off. As soon as I started getting down I got really skinny. I just wanted to read a book in the corner. I couldn't be bothered to dance for anyone unless they can pay me at least £400 ($550). And gradually people stopped wanting to pay me money.

Ronnie

AMÉLIE

I don't think I'm most of their types, like my outfits and stuff are so different to what they would normally come across. I often get, You look like the girl from *The Fifth Element*. I don't at all, but that's a great compliment. I think I just stand out a bit, I look a little bit like everything that they haven't explored. A lot of the girls just wear, you know, the sets – bra, suspender, knickers. I'm a bit more of a theatrical dresser. I always like to wear a body harness and stuff, or a ribbon around my neck so that I always have something on when I get naked. I'm a bit of a showgirl. Some girls just wear a one-piece and then that's all they have to take off. That wouldn't vibe with me because if I'm just doing a single dance, I tell them I'm not going to take off my knickers for, like, at least three dances. 'Cause you're not seeing my puss for £18 ($25). That's not happening. I've learned that it's up to you whether you take off your clothes or not.

I really enjoy dancing, that was the nicest thing about stripping. I really do love being amazed at what the female body has and, like, what it has over a hetero man. It's incredible. I remember when I got my first lap dance, like to show me how to do it, it blew my mind and I've always just tried to redo that. Everything is way slower than you'd think. It's all about how, wherever your eyes go, their eyes follow. Like, if I'm touching myself, but I'm keeping eye contact, they'll rarely look at my body if I've got the eye contact. And then if I look down, if I want them to look at my nipple or my hand on my arse, they'll follow it. It's kind of like when you point for a dog, the dog doesn't look at what you're pointing at, they look at your hand. It's like that but with your eyes for a man. I feel like that's such an incredible, empowering thing.

When I lead a customer upstairs, if they're walking behind me I hold their hand and I'm very slinky with my hips, because I'm just trying to dazzle them so much that they're a little bit spangled, and then they'll just give you all their money. I treat the first floor as my audition to try to get them upstairs to VIP, like just do such an amazing job that they have to go upstairs. I'll get them to sit against one of the chairs that has a wall just in case I topple, because these heels are really high and I'm actually quite clumsy. That's why there's a lot of floor work with me.

So they're sitting with their legs apart, and I always like to start off leaning forward over them, so they can sort of smell your warmth and the perfume on your neck. I don't have long hair, so it's not like I do any hair flicks or anything. It's about getting their face really close in that area that feels so intimate, like your neck and your shoulder. I'll always start with that because it's not just full tits and puss, it's a more sensual, intimate thing I think. Then, moving up, it's just sort of keeping their head really close to your space, but without ever touching them. It's like a spell. Then I'll turn around and just slowly bend down and look behind at them, while my hands go up my legs to my bum. From that I usually then bend forward to a crawl, and then it's kind of become my signature thing to go into the splits and then back up onto all fours. I'm like very slow and syrupy when I dance in VIP, which is completely different to when I'm actually out dancing, which is very jagged and buggy. But, yeah, then if they're lucky, maybe I'll start pulling down one of my straps and then just leave it there while I give a little bit more neck action again. I'll try not to take anything off on that first song if I can help it.

It's like when you're actually having sex or foreplay, if I want a guy to shag me and they're being a bit funny about it, I play with their hands or, you know, maybe touch their neck. Not things that are obvious. Because they might be like, I don't want this. And then you subtly show them that they *do* want this. It's like that, and as the song is about to finish, you just go, Shall we stay for another? Or, Shall we go upstairs? And they're like, Yeah, yeah, yeah!

.·.

Men go to strip clubs for an ego boost; for finding some weird connection. Going to a strip club isn't the same as going to a prostitute, there's no actual intercourse, so maybe it feels like it's okay, like it's allowed. For the rush of being a bit naughty and maybe the bragging rights of it. I think it's all very personal for each person. I think, for a lot of married men, it makes them feel like they're not doing anything wrong. Feeling special somewhere when they might not feel special very often. These are middle-aged guys that were probably a bit embarrassing at high school, so it's a validation thing and this is a very easy way to feel validated for a night. They're happy. I'm happy. There's no problem.

You're their mum and you're their slut at the same time. But you're not their wife. I had this one guy who was straight away, like Hey, let's go up to VIP! I'm like, Okay! And then he said, Um, actually I've got a confession, I just need to get this off my chest. I cheated on my wife from an arranged marriage of years and years with a sex worker recently. And at this stage I'm like straddling this guy, just sitting on him. That's basically all we did for like the next hour and a half or whatever. At the time I was actually seeing a therapist and I was like, *Do these guys know that there are professionals that can take care of them? Who know what they're talking about and for a lot less money?*

It's interesting because normally you'd meet these people and you'd just think, *Tory. They're all pricks. They're all dickheads.* But I think actually my work as a stripper has made me less judgemental. Because you just end up being therapists for everybody for so long that you just think like, people are just very lonely and it's quite sad.

Because we're strippers and not prostitutes, I think that it can almost be harder in some respect, because you're trying to keep someone's attention for so long without any payoff. Because people will go, Why the fuck would I spend that much money? Obviously I try to explain to them that it's an experience. Like, you're not just coming here to get your rocks off, you're coming here to be around a human being. Because otherwise you could just jerk off over the internet, couldn't you? You're wanting to have an interaction with someone. And you're having to keep them at this point of foreplay for possibly hours without them then getting frustrated and leaving and then being angry at you. Yeah, that's the hardest part about it, it's like *sustained stripping*. How the fuck do you do it?! It's something I'm still trying to learn. I have some really good customers but, you know, I really hit a wall after four hours. But you don't know when this is going to happen again, so you just keep going and then you come away feeling just absolutely drained. And I think that's the most exhausting part of stripping, keeping someone interested without providing any sex.

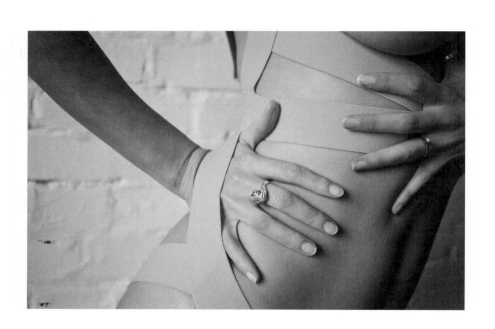

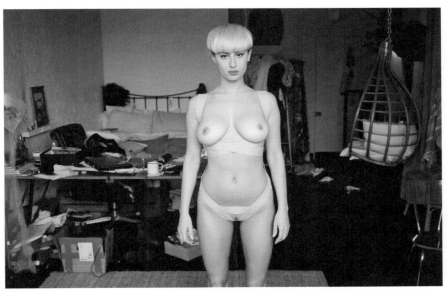

Amélie

SOPHIA

I can't just pick any name; it needs to be a powerful name. Names are really important. You can't be a Cinnamon or a Cookie or something stupid like that because the whole of your time there, you're just going to get bombarded with jokes that are just going to drive you mad. So it needs to be a simple, clear name that people won't really question. Sometimes I would even give myself a dancer name and then another fake name because that just gets rid of that conversation of, No really, what's your real name? Oh, my real name's Sarah. Oh, okay I believe that one.

So I had the name Sophia, which kind of suited me because people would think I was Arab, but I've had probably about five or six different dancer names. And they're usually just names that either I like because I know another dancer with that name and they were always a top earner, or that name just means money to me. Sometimes if I know a girl who's done really well, then I'll just take that name. Isn't that strange? That is strange, I know.

When I was really young I watched *Showgirls* on TV late at night, and that's when I first realised what stripping was. I was like, *What is this world!? I need to get into this world! I'm going to be just like that.* So that's what really got me thinking. Even now, I still want those costumes.

My dancer character is the same as how I am in real life. Sometimes that name will give me a bit of power here and there when I need it, but the character is me and that's just how I am. I think it's too hard to pretend to be someone else, because that is very draining and having to decompress from that is not worth the energy you put out, basically. I grew up doing musical theatre and going to theatre school, so I was always a dancer and a performer. Even like now when I'm on cam, it's hard for me to not have that performance persona. When I've tried to be natural, it's like, but naturally this *is* me! It's hard to not act when you've been taught to act your whole life. Also, I was coming out of being that cute, young theatre girl, and all of a sudden I'm sexy and people are looking at me differently. So I thought, *How do I transition this into now making money?* And you know, something that's gonna last for a long time.

I always knew about strippers and dancers, but I had the same old thing that everyone thinks. *Oh, they must be on drugs, like, why would you want to do that?!* And then when I realised, *Oh, they're doing it because it's fun, and you can make lots of money and there's loads of men and they're good looking.* Like, *Oh, okay, nothing wrong with that.* I find guys that have money and are older, just really attractive. I've always found older guys attractive, and a lot of the guys at work have been very good-looking, but maybe that's just my perception that I think they're good-looking, 'cause I think money is good-looking.

• •
•

Dancing on stage is my favourite part. I wish that we could just take it back to how it was in the 80s when it was more about the performance, before it got all about the guys trying to get as much as they could, like, they always need more. But so much of it is about the performance and there should always be a space for that because it's an artistic thing. It's the same thing with the camming. Like when you first start camming you realise, yeah there's loads of girls fingering themselves on cam, that's cool. But if you're the girl that *doesn't* do that, people are more interested because they can't get what they want and that's *way* more interesting, you know?

The private dances and the stage shows are completely different. The performance on stage is kind of like an interview, it's like giving a taster of what being with me is going to be like. But sadly, most of the time it doesn't actually matter. Because I would say it's probably only a tiny percentage of guys that are like, *Wow, you're amazing on stage, let me spend a thousand pounds on you.* No, it doesn't work like that. People just enjoy the entertainment of watching someone nice, but most of the guys that are spending all that money, they're not sat there watching the girl on stage. They're sat there trying to order a bottle of Champagne or maybe they've just gone straight to VIP. Personally, I think the stage shows are more for the dancer. If you want to make big money I don't think being on the stage is going to make any difference.

Do I enjoy the private dancing? Yes and no. Sometimes I would rather do the least dancing possible and just try to talk it out, which I normally do, I'll just cut straight to some kind of conversation that they're attracted to. As soon as I talk to a customer, straight away I'm trying to find that one thing that we are going to be talking about all night and he's going to be so happy that he spoke about it because he's been trying to talk about it for ages, but he didn't even know it. And I'm searching for it. Then before you know it, it's been three hours and I haven't even danced. That's what people don't understand, they think, *Oh, it's just this seedy thing where guys want to see girls naked.* No, it isn't. And I almost don't even want people to know what it *really* is because that might ruin it!

I'm quite good at analysing people, and I like to be the best. It's an ego thing I guess, but then it's to do with money as well. I want to make the most money out of everyone. Like, I need to get the most money that I can out of every situation. So maybe it's a money thing ... but wait, hang on ... sorry, I forgot the question 'cause I'm just thinking about money now... Oh yeah, so this is what I was going to say. When I first started working I realised it isn't how I thought it would be. You have to schmooze, you have to talk, you have to get in their head almost. You have to let them know that they're gonna spend all this money. And at first I used to go over to guys and say, Oh hey, do you want to dance? And as I'm saying that, I knew it was going to be, No. Like, maybe you'll get the odd guy, but that's just one dance, that's not going to serve me well. So when I realised that, I'd write down that thing I said, and then move on to something else entirely. I'd go through these different sequences to see what would work because so many things *didn't* work. And then when I found out what worked for me, I was like, okay, so now how do I ask for more money? So now when I'm in that situation, I'm like working off a script of things to say to get the most out of that situation. But now, it's sort of natural for me to just say to the guys what I need. But when I started there were so many things that didn't work for me and I didn't understand why – it's so easy to fall into the trap of repeating yourself and not learning from that.

∴

It's not about looks, it's about how that person's making you feel. You're ignorant if you think it's about that – people don't come here for looks. If someone is giving them that feeling that's taking them away from all the bullshit or whatever's going on in their life, that person can look absolutely beautiful to you. That person's giving you this feeling that you've never had, or probably haven't had in years. It's just the young, naive people that think, *Oh, it's just about looks*.

So for me, it doesn't matter who you are, what you look like, you're just money, in essence, to me. So I never judge. But now that I think about it, I would say that I make most of my money from the young sort of guys that are just there to party. I've never ever had long-term customers, ever. And that's because my customer is that young person that is just out going crazy that night. Or it's someone that didn't want to go crazy, and I've made them go crazy, why not, you know? Let's have fun.

In a sense, you do feel bad because these people are going in there drinking, partying, spending all their money and I guess, yeah, in your head, you're thinking, *Well, that money could have gone to something else*. You do feel bad for that, but then a part of you is like, *Well you shouldn't go in there anyway*. When I'm talking to them I know that they can't say no, so I have to take some responsibility. And sometimes when I get home, I'm just like, *Oh God, I can't even think about it*. Or, like, sometimes they'll tell me some really deep, weird secret they've probably never told anyone before. It's a lot to take on knowing that you're the only person that they've told this to. And then you're thinking, I wonder how they feel about that. They're probably shitting themselves thinking, *Oh bloody hell I can't believe I told that girl that thing I've been hiding for years*.

Then there's also the other thing of really finding out what men are truly like. Or some types of men – I shouldn't say all men because it doesn't really give you much trust in men when you hear about these stories. About how these guys are tempted by other women and how some of them are like, Oh, I've got a wife at home and she's pregnant, but I'd love to fuck you tonight. And I'm just thinking, *Oh God I'd love to just tell your wife right now, I would literally love to just ring her up and tell her.* But then there's sometimes guys that are like, My dog died 20 years ago and I'm still upset about it. And you just want to ring their wife and be like, Oh, he's such a sweet guy.

I probably do know too much, yeah. Maybe sometimes it's best to be more naive, but I guess it's sort of given me an insight, as in, now I know what to look out for in potential men in my life. And personally, to be honest with you, I wouldn't want to date a guy that went to strip clubs. And obviously when you're a dancer and you get that one guy that's like, No, no dances for me, I've got a wife at home, sorry. That's the guy you want to have as your husband or boyfriend.

.   .
 .

I've never looked down on them. I feel bad for them. I feel bad that they have to hide this massive part of their life, that they're so stressed out and so depressed throughout their whole life that they have to be horrible to us, because they've got no one else to be horrible to. Even when a guy is swearing at me or saying that they want to fucking murder a woman or something weird like that, I never look down on them. I actually feel sorry for them. I feel bad for them. I don't want them to feel that life's hit them so bad that the only thing they can do is go to a strip club and be angry at women.

When it's just you and one customer, people don't know what he's saying to you. He could be whispering in your ear, Oh, I'd love to murder you. Some people say weird shit like that. Honestly, sometimes when guys are drunk they become like the devil, and some of them also like to play the race thing, especially with me. They'd be like, Oh, I hate Black women. You know, Black this or Black that, and I'd be like, *Okay, well he clearly knows that I'm mixed.* It's like they would want to torture you almost. Or this one time with my friend, she's full Black, and these guys were like, Oh, let's play Brianna

Taylor. You can be her and I'll be the cop that killed you. And I'm like, how far is this going to go?! It's madness. Sometimes they're just saying it because they want the shock factor. They like to scare you because that's what gets them off. And that's why they'd always go for me because you could tell me something really horrendous, or you could tell me something really funny, and I'd always just be like, Oh okay, cool. That's why I'd always get those customers. They'd push and push and push and I'd still just be like, Hehehe. I feel like a lot of them go out looking for the vulnerable girls. They want that vulnerability; they want to take it away and do something really scary because that's what they get their enjoyment from.

It's as if someone has given you an insight into human behaviour and what people are really like when they don't think anyone's watching. You learn so much about men, about money, about egos. And also about being street smart, 'cause customers are always trying to trick you – they've paid or they haven't paid, or they've cancelled their card … it's like express learning into human behaviour. Like, I look at my younger cousins who are only five, six years younger than me, they have no experiences compared to me. That's what it is, it's the different personalities and how people present themselves, and then what they *really* turn into, you can see that all in the space of one night. It just goes to show that someone can be portraying themselves to be one way, and then by the end of it, they've completely broken down and they're someone else entirely, and no normal person would think that's even possible until you've seen it, been there, heard it. Maybe that could be seen as a bad thing, but I think it's actually a really good thing. The bad thing is the fact that you get trapped thinking that life is only about money, and it's very addictive because you know you can always just go back to it. It becomes a way of life. It's almost like when someone goes to prison and they get so used to it, so they want to go back because that's what they're comfortable with.

I've been dancing since I was 18 and I'm 31 now. Too long. And I would have carried on doing it for like the next four or five years. But now I need to just be smarter. I need to be smarter because I've managed to make the same money working on cam, and I'm doing less hours, I'm less stressed and I'm not driving back and forth and feeling drained. I'm in my own environment doing what I want to do, and if you don't like it, you can leave the room, you know? There's obviously something nice about being in the club, but I don't really like being around alcohol and that drunk environment. It's a lot of like, broken people that are searching for something. I didn't want to admit it to myself that cam is actually really good, but when you think about it, it's online so there's more people there. It's limitless, it's 24 hours. I could log on right now and someone would be there. Like, it's definitely the way forward, but it's a shame because what does that mean for strip clubs? Maybe strip clubs should just go back to how they were, just for actual entertainment, for like proper shows and performances.

LORELEI

GISELLE

AMY

KATIE

CLEO

AMÉLIE

CHIQUI

CHANGING

ROOMS

There's something about the conditions of working in a strip club that inspire enduring female friendships. You might imagine that so many women hustling in a competitive environment would create all manner of feuds and grudges, and you'd be right. But what most dancers seem to remember more vividly are the alliances.

Some of the friendships might seem quite unlikely. We're thrown together with women we might not cross paths with in the normal course of our lives: women of different nationalities, subcultures and social groups. We might not always share a primary language, but there's a shared sense of being together and doing this strange job that places us outside the normal streams of everyday life. What most strippers recall is the camaraderie.

Perhaps it's to do with being naked together that breaks down the barriers of reserve. After seeing yourself and everybody else reflected from every angle in the mirrored changing room for so long, nudity starts to feel normal, as do all sorts of other intimacies and private rituals. We feel safe enough to talk frankly about ourselves and our bodies – there's little space for embarrassment in the changing room.

On busy shifts, it's always bustling with girls vying for space in front of the mirrors. Every surface is littered with stripper detritus: transparent shoes, random lingerie items, cosmetics, baby wipes, and body lotions. It's the place where we carry out so many of the personal operations most people would do in private ... extracting an ingrown pubic hair or flossing our teeth etcetera.

This restorative space, away from the gaze of the customers, is also a sanctuary where we escape the floor, share inside jokes, eat, and recharge. The conversations that take place within these sequestered spaces are the funniest, most animated we've ever had. But it's also an antidote to any ideas you might once have entertained about strip clubs being glamorous. Enveloped by the smell of various meals reheated in the communal microwave, the sensory overwhelm of multiple conversations, and the sound of someone playing frenetic Romanian chart music on their phone, being in the changing room is like glimpsing behind the wizard's curtain; any whiff of glitz or mystery is extinguished, yet it's somehow even more alluring.

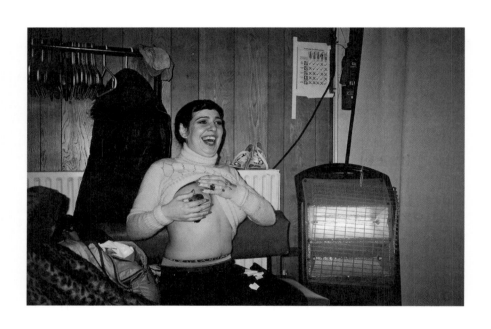

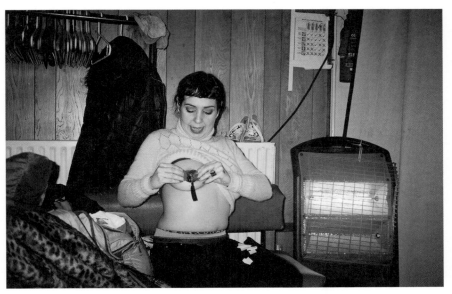

Lucy

LORELEI

The changing room conversations are the best I've ever had in my life. I wish we recorded some of them to look back on. If someone ever put a secret camera there, man, you know, you could write books on them. Best chats ever. I've learned so much from the changing room.

One funny conversation actually ... we were in the changing rooms downstairs. And, you know, you always have these customers who try to save you. Did someone hurt you? Were you abused as a kid? You know, all this. We all got those guys here and there. This one time, a girl came downstairs and she said, Oh, this guy, he just asked me if I had daddy issues. And, you know, we've heard that, we've all heard it. So we were just sitting there laughing. *They're* the ones that have the problem! And then I was like, So where's your dad? She's like, Oh, I've never known him. And the other girl said, Oh no, me and my dad haven't spoken since I was three. And I was like, Well, I grew up without one. And then we're all sitting there thinking, *Hmm, maybe there* is *something to this daddy issues thing.* So funny.

GISELLE

I didn't like getting ready at home before I got to work. For me, there was something about being in the changing room. I liked arriving really early so I had time to just breathe into it and get ready. You'd feel your posture changing as it got closer to the time to go out. I'd be very conscious, walking out from the changing rooms. I timed it. I'd wait till just after someone had finished their stage show so people were starting to look around a bit more, then I'd walk out and not look anyone in the eye until someone caught my attention, then I'd sort of give them a coy smile but keep walking. And you'd hear the flutter of, Who's she? And so you'd just feel that power of, like, *Right, I've created something of a buzz here.* The little manipulations, the small things – it's all so, so calculated.

I wasn't Giselle unless I'd got on the lingerie and fake tan. If I didn't have fake tan on, my self-confidence plummeted. It was like Photoshopping yourself before you went out on stage. That's something that changed a lot over the course of the 15 years I did it. When I started, nobody really wore fake tan and nobody looked anything like they look these days. Makeup has changed so much, in a way, and people are expected to look Photoshopped a lot more. But Photoshop didn't exist in 2000, you know, so you'd see some people who looked really, like, what by Kardashian standards these days would look really fucking ropey. But it was just how people looked. Now there's become a sort of homogenisation, everybody's aspiring to look exactly the same.

Striptease did used to be subversive. It's so fucking commonplace now. Things like Instagram, I think, have had a huge impact. Just everyone wanting to basically look the same. And it's too much of a risk for strip clubs at the moment to try to be innovative and different because, who is their market? And if we're being more open about ideas of gender and performances of gender as well, the traditional strip club just doesn't have any room for otherness. So, actually, the range of people they're marketed to has become narrower and narrower and narrower, and they're offering less and less but trying to charge more. They're such a perfect representation of capitalist myopia, it's amazing. I always thought this, about strip clubs being a wonderful economic barometer, actually, because they're so tied up to the City of London.

I think, yes, it's changed a lot. And the whole atmosphere has just become a lot more competitive and eventually it will, I think, bust. And then it might be able to grow back up into something new and much more subversive and interesting again.

Anna

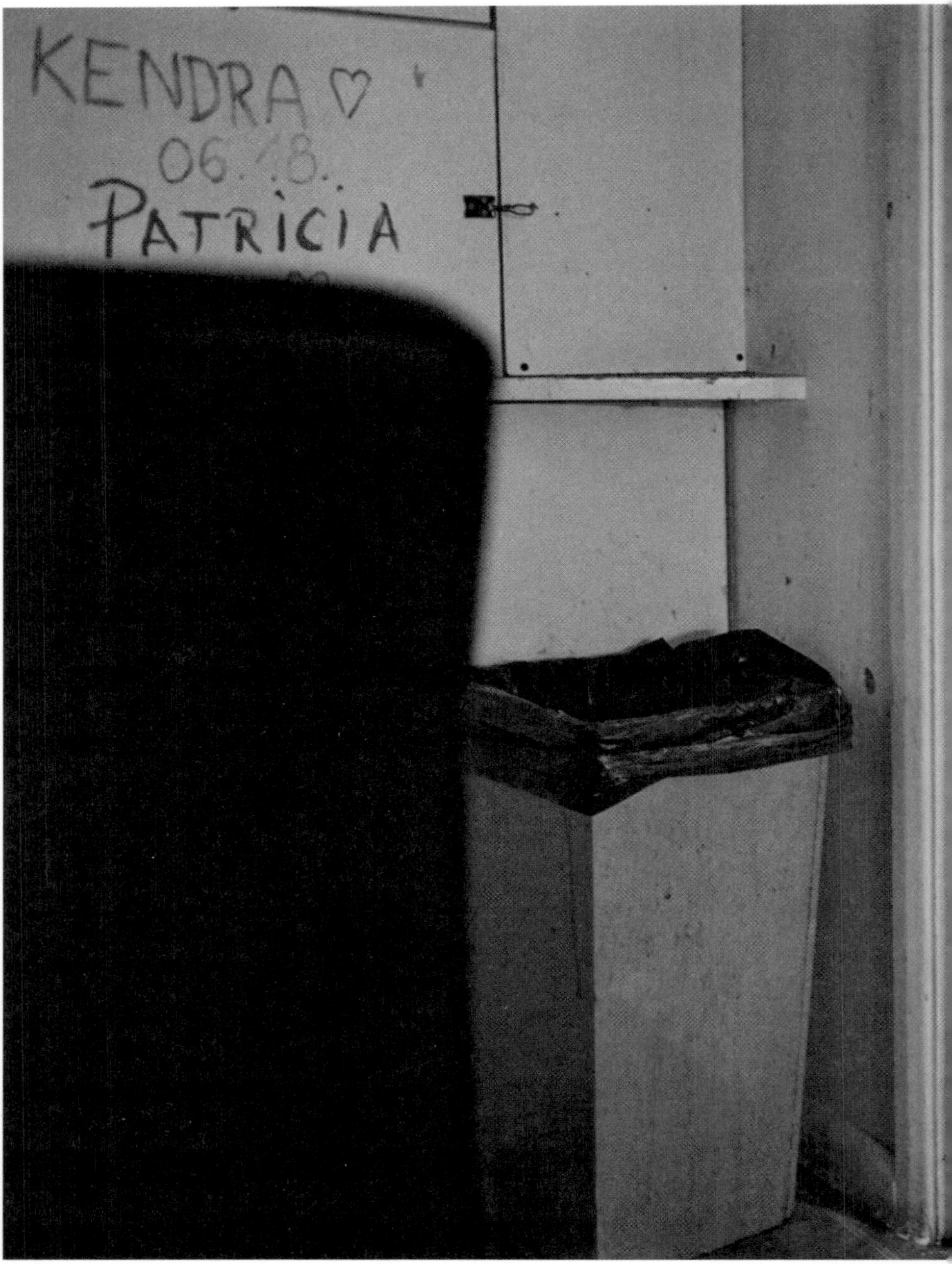
KENDRA ♡
PATRICIA

Bex

AMY

I've worked in loads of different industries and I haven't met the kind of special women that I've met in that club. The best thing that happened to me is the three or four women I met there who literally gave me support in all areas – creatively, emotionally; people that I consider real friends, which I don't think I really had before. I think that comes from understanding that in a lot of environments – nightclubs, club scenes – women are competing, using their sexuality, competing for attention from men. But *we're* not competing for attention, we want *money*. It's not about putting each other down, it's about, *Right, we're here for a reason.* So when you're at a normal party and you see another woman and you can feel they're in competition with you, they're performing their sexuality for a male gaze, it's just like, *Pfffffft, you're missing the whole point here.* It's just like you got this other understanding of patriarchy. It's a deeper understanding of what's going on logistically, and how they manage to exert power over us and how they manage to play women off of each other.

I think it's always a very certain sector of male society that goes there. There's a very high percentage of men that wouldn't go in there, you know, like even my boyfriend when he's on a stag do. I'm like, When you go to a strip club make sure you spend £100 ($140), don't go in there and fuck about. And he's like, Yeah, but it's fake. And I was like, I don't care, if you're going in those spaces then spend money. That's a real massive pet hate of mine, is men that are in there to get everything they can for their money. It's disgusting. I love men that come in there and are really generous and know the etiquette of what's happening and they're grateful, and they understand that that's what we deserve to have. As soon as someone starts twitching about money I just walk away from them. I'm like, *No.* I'd rather earn nothing than sit here and try to extract £25 ($35) out of you in three hours.

I think some girls definitely have got that, like ... they've channelled into something. I'd say it's 'affect' – you know there's that whole theory of 'affect'? It's kind of like a philosophy around what happens between people, the energies happening between people all the time. A lot of queer studies talk about it, and I feel like some girls understand that philosophy and they know how to touch someone or what to say, it's very instinctual. And it's a gift, you know. Affect talks a lot about charisma, like what is charisma? What was it that Hitler had or what Marilyn Monroe had; we haven't really got words for it. And there's some girls that have that, and they can read people and they know what people want. And they don't have a type, it could be anyone, and they know what to do. And that's amazing.

What I've come to realise now is, I'm not gonna make my fortune as a stripper. I kind of thought, *I'll be able to earn this money, save it, get a house, do a degree.* But I need to decide who I am gonna be, so that means the stripping bit has to go because it's like any job, you just have to commit. And that's why I really respect a couple of girls there, you know, they keep themselves so trim. I know during the day they go to the gym, be health freaks, meditate, get in that space, then in the week they're like *boom boom boom cash cash cash.* And they've got a plan and that's what they want to do and I really respect that. It is their career. You can't knock it, but it's not my career. It's definitely a chapter in my life and it's a chapter that I'm really, really grateful that I've had the opportunity to do. I've learnt so much, I've learnt so much about my sexuality, about my desire, about my boundaries, about men, about patriarchy, about the male gaze, about friendship, about women. I've learnt loads.

Amy

Amy

KATIE

Meeting a new friend can sometimes feel like falling in love, like a romance.

The first time I saw Frankie was at my audition at ███ █████. I'd decided to become a stripper having never, ever performed in any capacity on a stage in my life, apart from, you know, being in school nativity plays and hating it and freezing, mortified. I would try to hide at the back in any PE class, and I never even danced when I went out with my friends. I was really, really self-conscious – riddled with self-consciousness. But, because there was a side to me that was drawn to the sleazier side of life, I thought it would be a good idea to be a stripper. The thought of going up on a stage, occupying it and performing in front of an audience – not so much even taking my clothes off, but like, the actual idea of having to be confident and have all those people staring at me – was my worst nightmare. And it's still one of the scariest things I've ever done.

Frankie was working on that shift when I did my audition and she came to the front of the stage and stood watching me. And I was just absolutely burning with shame, like, having no idea how to be sexy on stage but instantly recognising that she was just innately cool and sexy. I was 25 but, looking back, I don't even think I was really ... I don't think I knew my own self or really had a proper sense of my own sexual powers, let alone performing being sexual onstage. I was less bothered about the men in the audience watching me because, you know, I had really great tits and I knew that they would be much more forgiving of me not doing very much dance-wise and just taking my clothes off. But the idea of the other women watching – especially her because I immediately thought she just looked so cool – I just found really mortifying. I was so bad on stage I'm amazed I got a job. I must have looked so afraid, I just couldn't conceal how nervous I was.

Frankie had this gravelly Essex accent that I came to love. And she was always changing her appearance or getting tattoos, even though the owner hated the girls having tattoos. She was always dyeing her hair different colours – she was quite experimental with the way she looked. She was sort of alternative-looking, but not in an obvious goth or metal kind of way.

Becoming friends with her happened gradually as I started coming out of my shell a little bit more. I was clearly a total rookie, but she never patronised me. I've always been one of those people, I think, maybe, that people want to take under their wing – certain types of people. I don't know if it's because I've got a very, like, soft voice, it's a bit childlike. I think it's quite misleading because my sense of humour is quite dark, and I can be quite sarcastic. But I have this thing about me where in social situations my survival instinct is to not really reveal myself in that way and to just be overly nice and soft to please people.

I remember when she started giving me a lift home after late shifts. She was the same age as me but she just seemed so much more worldly wise. And I remember that I couldn't even drive at this point, but she had this Mercedes convertible. Frankie had already been a dancer for, like, eight years by that time. She owned a flat and had this car and she was a bit of an old hand, even though we were the same age. I think it was on these lifts home that I was able to gradually relinquish this persona that I had created to sort of insulate myself.

Frankie was so bold and very confident about her own self and her opinions, but she also was funny, and funny at her own expense – she could laugh at herself. And nothing really was off the table to laugh at, it didn't matter how dark or how out of order something was ... sad things, tragic things, it was all very available to laugh at. And there's so much to laugh at, in a strip club.

She was incredibly poised on stage; she would move really slowly and confidently. She had been a gymnast when she was a teenager so she had this very toned, flexible body and she would do these incredible, controlled moves that just made her seem so confident. And she would make a lot of eye contact. But she was also just really irreverent and funny. She could be this smouldering character, but then the next minute she would completely undermine that by laughing at herself. Her sense of humour was self-deprecating, but she would also turn it on other people as well, especially customers.

Frankie was incredibly intelligent, not like academically so, but she was really sharp and quite shrewd. I felt that she lived in the moment, whereas I was someone who had been through a much more rigorous kind of education, academically, and I lived in my head. She was more ruled by her emotions. I was totally guided by a kind of abstract thought process that would always take me out of the moment, whereas she was really present.

I loved working with her; the first thing I did when I got the week's rota was check which days we were working together. We were a good team. Frankie was much more upfront and she would joke with the customers and kind of take the piss out of them. My instinct was much more to kind of avoid talking about money, to just instinctively try to flatter them and anticipate what they liked and allow them to project that on me. Whereas you couldn't really project anything onto her.

That friendship was maybe amplified by the environment we were in because things are more intense and intimate. For instance, there's less privacy about bodily functions or any of the more embarrassing private sides of what it means to occupy a body. We would laugh about her having piles, and she would call them Piley Cyrus. Or talking about periods, sex, etc. You know, our sense of humour was much cruder – probably because of the job – so there was no prudishness and it was like nothing was too gross to laugh about.

I don't remember one major incident that cemented our friendship. It was more, for me, like these incremental moments of me stepping out from this persona that I'd spent years creating as a way to avoid being rejected, or, I don't even know … but I'd spent a long time crafting this way of being in the world that was about not really showing who I was. And so it was like, tip-toeing outside of that and daring to say something that maybe other people disagreed with, or daring to be myself and feeling that she actually welcomed it and, if anything, liked me more for it. It was more like that than being some big turning point. But we definitely had tons and tons of nights where we were doing sit-downs making loads of cash, or where we were having a shit night and not earning any money and just hanging out in the changing rooms, just kind of, you know, sitting around and entertaining ourselves. And these inhibitions I'd spent the past 25 years building were just gradually being dismantled.

I think I have been able to bring a bit of Frankie's energy into my other friendships as I've got older, and been able to be more uninhibited, and also to feel more confident and reveal aspects of myself that I would normally have only revealed to people I was really, really comfortable with. And to value my anomalies rather than just sort of do what I did at school, which was have this very rich inner life reading books and listening to music and watching films, spending a lot of time in junk shops going through old vinyl and old Elvis Presley fan club magazines and ephemera – all these interests I had that were not … that were considered weird by my most of the people I went to school with. I had this world that I kept for myself, and within myself, living in my own head and rarely bringing that out into the real world. So I think it was a really transformative kind of friendship, in a way. Probably less so for her because she was already so much herself. But I was a good foil to her.

And she, in her own world, I think, was a bit of an anomaly, probably. In her own way, she was a little bit of a deviant, I think. Not in the way that we understand deviancy as, like, something really extreme or subversive or violent, but in the sense that she deviated from the norm. And I think I did too, and that we, like, recognised that about each other.

I think my friendship with Frankie hasn't been able to exist in the same way outside of the space of the strip club, as much as we would both like it to and as much as we're both really, really fond of one another. I think it's partly because we both have kids now and we don't live close to each other, so we're busy. And we kind of live in different worlds. But I think when you say 'friends of circumstance' that sounds diminishing. We haven't actively stayed in touch, though when we have spoken over the years since we both stopped dancing, we are right back there.

I think our friendship is about maybe being in that environment together. And it doesn't always work to take a friendship out
of that scenario and pop it into this different setting with different
people who don't have that shared experience. And, yeah, it doesn't
mean anything less of the friendship, it doesn't mean that it's not a
really powerful kind of relationship. But just that it flourishes in that
particular environment.

Our shared memories have been some of the best memo-
ries we have in our lives, I think it's like that for both of us. You know
the things you have with old friends – the shared language, the little
in-jokes that have evolved so much they would be impossible to
explain to someone else because they've gone through so many
permutations, and involve so much context.

But we just haven't really been able to keep up that, you
know, sort of everyday relationship where you're seeing each other
and you're knowing what's going on in the day-to-day running of
one another's lives. We've never become a part of the fabric of
each other's normal life. It's like, our friendship, even as intense
and important as it was, is sort of contained in that time. I think we'll
always periodically get back in touch, but most of our conversation
will be about recounting memories of things that have happened in
the past.

She was just so charismatic. And yeah, I felt really proud to
be friends with her if you know what I mean? And I never felt jealous
of or competitive with her. And I felt like that about a lot of girls that
I really cared about at work – I didn't feel like I was competing with
them. I felt really proud to be on the same team. I felt like ... sorry, I feel
really emotional talking about this.

Amber & Venus

Honey

CLEO

I enjoy the unpredictability of work. I enjoy the stories that I take home, and it's not mundane. No day is the same. I really enjoy the company of the girls. I find that they have a fucking brilliant sense of humour and a lot of the women that I meet there are so fucking resilient and they come from all different backgrounds. Some of them come from really tough backgrounds, some of them are just like middle-class girls, some come from Brazil where members of their family have been shot. But we all have this camaraderie and that's a really fucking cool thing to be a part of. I think there's a certain closeness that you have with other dancers because you kind of support one another in this environment that other people can't understand. Because how could you possibly understand it unless you're in it. So that definitely forges some kind of mutual understanding of one another.

The bits I don't enjoy are the nights where you don't make money and maybe you're on your period and not feeling particularly great about yourself. And then on top of that some customer tells you that you look like you could use a fucking facelift and starts grabbing fat on your body and saying awful things about your appearance.

It's interesting though, because working as a stripper, you realise that there's no normal body type, everyone's body is just so different. Customers have either loved my tits or criticised them. Everybody just likes different things and what one person sees as beautiful another person will see as a flaw. But I definitely have less hang-ups about my body than I used to. Quite significantly. I've just learned to accept my body through being around other people who accept their bodies. There are things that I would be insecure about in my body, but I'll see someone else who has a very similar feature and they seem to love it or use it to their advantage. So it just gives you a different perspective on the way that you look at yourself.

The thing that really irritates me the most is shaving my vagina, because I would always be inclined not to have it completely bald. But in some clubs, like ███████ for example, the house mum is like, You know men like it. And basically they're telling you, you should shave it all off. But it fucking hurts to shave it all the time, it's really fucking uncomfortable. And you can't wax it because you don't have enough time to grow it out. I just think it's so much sexier to have some hair. I don't like the bald vagina look; I think it looks really infantile and I find it strange that this is what's generally regarded to be sexy. I think that it has a lot to do with porn. But I've started to give less of a shit, so I'm not perfectly shaven anymore, and I don't shave my legs because they're not going to fucking touch my legs anyway.

Switching between the roles of your normal self and your weird nocturnal self, it can be a bit of a mind-fuck sometimes. And sometimes I have to just take a few weeks off, especially if I work a lot, because I feel like I've lost touch with who I really am. I become this weird creature who runs around at night being crazy in this pretty surreal environment, then I wake up in the day and I'm like, *Who the fuck am I?!* It's not like you just come home, put your bag down and put the TV on. It's almost like you have to come to terms with what you've just soaked in. I think you have to be quite receptive and quite emotionally open to be good at the job, so you do end up taking on a lot of people's shit. And it can be pretty exhausting.

I think I've had periods before where I stopped dancing for the wrong reasons, like maybe because I had a jealous boyfriend. But I always knew I'd go back to it, and I missed it. But I hope that eventually I will make money from doing what I really love to do; the creative things I do. Then I probably won't be stripping but I'll definitely fucking miss it because I do love the job. You know, it's really entertaining to me.

Barbara

AMÉLIE

I feel like everything's heightened. It's the same with your relationships with other dancers. It's such an intense environment that if you get on with someone, you *really* get on with them, and if you don't get on with someone, you *really* don't get on with them. It's interesting. It's like high school sort of, you know? There's the older girls that sort of feel like, you know, you're on their turf, so you've got to pay your dues and stuff. Initially I was a bit like, *Yeah, sure, I'm happy to please and be a puppy dog.* Then, after a while, I was just like, *No, bitch. I've paid my dues, you've paid yours, everybody's fucking equal. I don't care if you've been working here since you were 18. I didn't do that. Sorry.*

Everyone used to stick to the rules but then it got a bit lawless. It would be okay if everybody was making money but, if people aren't, then everybody starts going a bit fucking mental. It can get quite gross, I hate that vibe, but I understand. 'Cause everybody's just stressed, you know? But the thing I hate the most is when dancers are like, I've got bills to pay. And it's like, yeah, we all do. That's why we're at work. Some people have kids and some people don't, it doesn't make one person's way of earning money more or less important. Just be quiet, please. You chose to drive all the way from fucking Essex, don't complain about it to me. I don't know why you're making it everybody else's issue. I don't really have much sympathy with that. I have sympathy for, you know, when you're not making any money and it is stressful. I do understand that. But some people will just perpetuate that negative energy as well, and I'm just like, *Get away from me.*

..
.

WANTING YOU TO WANT ME

I'm keen to go back to it if it's not completely dead but, because of Brexit, the industry has quietened down a lot. At least for our club, 'cause it's in the City. If they're freaking out about what's going to happen with the pound and euros and stuff, they're not spending money, and that's where it hits directly for us. Our customers are like high-powered dudes in the banks and private equity and stuff. So it did change a lot. My first year dancing, I was just like, *Oh my God, I've never made this much money in my life!* And I was just splashing it everywhere, like Ubers all the time, Uber to infinity. But the following year I had basically halved what I had earned from the first year and was almost on like minimum wage. So it did change a lot.

And, like I said earlier, the club vibe changed and I feel like it's really sad because it's got such a potential to be, like, rather than women against women, it could be women against the men. We've got the power. We can do it and it's possible but, you know, the patriarchal system is just so ingrained in so many of us and we have to unlearn it. So that's the saddest part about it.

What do I miss most? I miss the power. That's probably the most honest answer. I miss the power, not even the money, I just miss the power. I mean, the money is pretty important, but some people are really driven purely by the money. And I am very driven by the show and the power from performance. I like the accolade. For a long time I was trying to push it down and be like, *No, no, no, I don't want to be on the stage, I just want to be behind the scenes, I don't want to act or anything.* Because I had this weird notion that it was a really vacuous thing to want. And then I had a click moment a couple of years ago when I was dancing, I was like, *Why have I been trying to hide away? This is just who I am.* I'm such a show-off! I always have been, and that's fine. That's not a bad thing. I like attention from everyone. I'm not biased about your gender. *Just give me all of your attention.* Like, really, ultimately we do want everyone to like us. Most of us do. It's pretty much the human condition, I think. I've only really recently started being honest about it, that I just want everyone to like me. I want people to think I'm funny and enjoyable to be around.

Amélie

CHIQUI

I think I'm super blessed with the amount of amazing women I have met through this industry. You've seen each other drunk, you've seen each other on drugs, you've seen each other crying because a customer said you were ugly. So you see each other in such vulnerable positions and completely stripped, not only of your clothes. You expose parts of your personality that you wouldn't show to society normally, and that creates such a strong bond. You know, we're checking each other's tampon strings in the changing room. Once you've done that, and you've seen somebody putting glitter on their butthole, I think every boundary is broken.

There's no way you're not going to relate to these women somehow, because it's a complete striptease of *everything*. You also get to see how strong women are, because you have to be strong for this industry. The number one thing you're going to get in this job is rejection. You know, like how many rejections do you have to get through before you get a yes for a private dance? So that makes you really fucking strong and that makes you take no shit. Even the girls that I haven't particularly liked so much, I still admire how strong they are, and I still admire how they have put a big finger up to society. Like, *Fuck it, I'm going to sell the beauty of my body because I need fucking money and fuck what you think about me.* That takes a lot of guts.

It's like a family, you know, a sisterhood. I wouldn't change this for one thing. The deepest, strongest relationships I ever had have been with my fellow sex worker friends, for sure. There's no judgement, like who are we to judge? And there's no editing, you don't have to lie about who you are, you don't have to lie about your needs, you don't have to lie if a customer was rude to you. Because sometimes society is like, *Oh, well it's because you're a stripper, you put yourself in the situation.* A stripper will never tell you that shit. And that's why you really cherish these friends.

WANTING YOU TO WANT ME

I also think it's like a witch thing. It's very coven-like when women get together to play with the energy of sex, money, desire and therapy. Because let's not forget that we're healers. We're healing parts of our body, we're healing other people, we're healing female sexuality that has been punished for centuries. We are healing our self-worth because society says you're too fat, too skinny, you're ugly, I wouldn't fuck you ... but I'm making money out of this. It gives you this really raw self-esteem. I also think there's something quite magical and witchy about a bunch of girls getting together and smelling each other's periods. If one got their period, then suddenly all of us started – our bodies were so close together that we're smelling each other's hormones the whole time. There is something quite magical about that. I'm pretty sure it's very common, like it's probably the core of witchcraft. When women get together like this, we're creating magic.

Barbara

For Barbara.

With special thanks to Aurelia Butler,
Clément Cachot-Coulom, Abi Fellows, Eve Marleau,
Ruby Russell, and Jake Walters. And most of all to the
extraordinary women who appear in these pages.

Published in 2022 by Hardie Grant Books,
an imprint of Hardie Grant Publishing

Hardie Grant Books (London)
5th & 6th Floors
52–54 Southwark Street
London SE1 1UN

Hardie Grant Books (Melbourne)
Building 1, 658 Church Street
Richmond, Victoria 3121

hardiegrantbooks.com

British Library Cataloguing-in-Publication Data. A catalogue
record for this book is available from the British Library.

Wanting You to Want Me
ISBN: 978-1-78488-466-6

10 9 8 7 6 5 4 3 2 1

Publisher: Kajal Mistry
Commissioning Editor: Eve Marleau
Design: Stuart Hardie
Copy Editor: Isla Ng
Proofreader: Lucy Kingett
Production Controller: Nikolaus Ginelli

Colour reproduction by p2d
Printed and bound in China by Leo Paper Products Ltd.